A Baggage Car with Lace Curtains

By Kay Fisher

Black & White sketches by Robert Church, Wilton, California

Cover design, Mike Pinter, Grass Valley, California

Photo restoration, Heritage Graphics, Rancho Cordova, California

Printed by Allert & Bassett, Grass Valley, California

Published by

B & K FISHER · P.O. BOX 714 · COLFAX, CA 95713

Preface

This is a true story. The people are real. We have changed the names and identities, rearranged them if you will, because a few still work for the railroad and are our friends, though most have passed on. Each is an individual like someone you know, but all have one facet which makes them a little different — they are railroaders. As you read the book you will realize that each one was affected, as we were, by a way of life known as railroading.

The candid reader will recognize that all of us are influenced, indeed educated in our daily lives by the people among whom we live. The young reader may understand how things have changed; how life before welfare, TV or job security built qualities of self-reliance into young couples who now have become grandparents.

The rail buff will savor the era of great steam locomotives and recognize the territory. He will live with us beside the smoke, the hot odors, the pounding wheels and crashing exhausts that now have been stilled. The Mallets, Consolidations, the graceful Mountain type engines come to life, so close in fact he will feel their heat and sense the tremendous steam pressure in their massive boilers.

We hope you enjoy this account of our experiences in A Baggage Car With Lace Curtains.

1. The First Shock

The highway curved and climbed steadily between the mountains. On both sides of the road clusters of small Christmas trees stood closely at attention bolstered by their parents, a forest of stately firs behind them. We passed a sign, Elevation 5000 ft. Our 1938 Buick hummed along confidently because Bill had tuned the motor. Far ahead, across the horizon, a massive bulwark of granite peaks divided off the world.

"Bill, the scenery is like a painting!" I declared.

"Huh? Oh, great. I told you it would be." He'd been driving in silence with that world-on-his-shoulders look. "Kay, I hope we are doing the right thing, moving you up here. It's a different life up in these mountains. You'll have to adjust to a big change."

"We've decided to try it," I reminded him. "It can't be worse than being apart six days out of seven. Those Sundays were so terribly short."

"Like being married one day a week."

Our six months old marriage license was in my purse along with the car payment book. The back seat was loaded with boxes of clothing and groceries, our mattress and bed tied on top of the car. In my lap I held a precious package, a carefully wrapped ceramic coffee pot. It was a cobblestone design with a Dutch girl on it and to me it was a symbol of love, the first gift from my husband.

"Look, there is the railroad," Bill pointed out.

The road now skirted the edge of a canyon and below was a long graceful sweep of double tracks. I exclaimed, "Look at the houses down there, just stuck to the hillside."

"That's Emigrant Gap. We worked there just last week. Lot of snow here in winter, but we will be down to lower elevations by then. Maybe close to home."

Home was a little honeymoon cottage that had seen some turbulence during the first months of our marriage as we struggled to make ends meet. Then Bill had landed a railroad job that offered security and a future, but there was a ladder system called seniority and you had to start at the bottom. So he was assigned to a traveling job with living quarters in something called an 'outfit car' up here in the mountains. He had to batch all week with his helper, a young fellow named "Thatch", and could get home only late on Saturday. Sunday evenings we'd say goodbye as he left for another long week. That was the bad part.

Bill had suggested that I move up with him so we could be together, but we'd have to accept his helper who would be eating with us and staying in one section of the living car.

We had lost sight of the tracks now and were traveling alongside a sparkling stream with scattered summer cabins in beautiful little coves. Our own cute cottage was miles behind but I could still go back to it. The rent was paid for two more weeks.

"Cisco," Bill announced. He pulled off at a campground with a small store and post office, then turned up a steep graveled road that wound between the largest trees I'd ever seen. He shifted to second and then to low gear.

I didn't want to go back. Those long days alone, waiting for him to get home Saturday nights...the few desperate hours through Sunday...loving him as much as I could. It hadn't worked. Our marriage was not real, a struggle instead of happiness. It could collapse before it got started. Camping out in a railroad car might not be too bad. We'd be together every night and I could love him again. I was determined to try it.

But the deep forest shadows left by a sun now lost behind the mountains were a little frightening in this huge silent world. Streets, stores and traffic seemed far away, non-existent.

"Well, we're here," he reported. The road ended in a lonely wide spot with several parked cars. He put his arm around me tightly. "You'll like it up here, Kay-Kay. And I'll be able to kiss you every night." The way he said it sounded more like, 'We've taken the fort, my dear.'

He jumped out of the car and opened the door on my side. I was met by cool, clean, invigorating air and a bunch of very aloof fir trees. "Good thing it's still daylight," I declared. "What kind of animals are out there?"

"Only a few squirrels," he assured me. "The outfit cars are up there."

My eyes climbed a steep mountain. I could see a railroad grade cut into the slope far above us. No stairway was in sight.

"Nice easy trail," my Apache brave told me. "Let's get started. I'll come back for the bed and stuff."

"Bill, you can't carry our bed and mattress up there!"

"I'll get some help. You forget there is a track-laying gang up there, about sixty men." He shouldered a cardboard box and grabbed the suitcase, glowering when I insisted on carrying my coffee pot.

Nice easy trail! Brush scratched at my face, rocks rolled under my feet and gravel seeped into my shoes. It was like a stalled escalator down which somebody had poured a thousand marbles. With every lurch I thought the coffee pot was lost but I wouldn't admit that bringing it was foolish. I couldn't have talked anyway because I was breathing in gasps, while my husband strode smoothly ahead with both arms full. He turned around to find me hanging breathlessly onto a piece of brush.

"Better take a rest," he advised. "You make a lot of work out of it."

"I should have taken a course in mountain climbing! Bill, I don't think I can make it."

"Oh, sure you can. Take a blow and look at the scenery."

The canyon fell away below us. Far down we could hear trucks on the highway. Beyond, great jagged cliffs rose toward the sky in silent majesty-like chunks of world that had been left over. I would have been content to stand there and gaze but my husband started on. Slipping and sliding, I followed head down, breath wheezing.

He stopped suddenly. "There! Wasn't so bad, was it?"

We had reached a wide shelf like a boulevard laid with big shiny railroad tracks. Against the mountainside was a long chain of railroad cars on a side track. There were boxcars, coaches, flats, tank cars, all mixed, all a mud-red color and unimaginably old looking. Each had a ladder-like stairway propped against an open door. Dozens of men lolled on the steps and on the ground. The air carried mixed odors of fir trees, coal smoke and oil from the tracks. Behind the scene the mountain rose in silent disdain of the humans clinging to its slopes.

"This is the track gang," Bill explained. "Our outfit is farther up the spur." He started on, walking along the ties. The men ceased talking to gawk.

I stopped suddenly. "Dear, they're all Mexicans!"

"Sure," he agreed. "They'll be your friends by tomorrow."

"They'll be what?" I stood there with my coffee pot in one hand, my purse with our marriage license in the other. The license said I would love, cherish and obey this man, my husband, who was standing before all those grinning people, a string of decrepit railroad cars parked in the mountains, wondering what was wrong with me. "Dear," I said, "wait a minute."

"Aw, don't be afraid of them. Hiya, boys," he waved.

"Hi, Meester Beel," they chorused. "Como esta? Es la Senora?"

"O, si," Meester Beel grinned. To which they answered "Aha!" without taking their eyes off the new female arrival tripping along behind her husband and wondering if said husband wasn't slightly nuts to bring his six-month bride into wilds like this. Where the pathetic train of old cars ended Bill turned across the tracks.

"This is our outfit," he announced. "The 713 and boxcar 787."

It was a high, old wooden baggage car with six windows and a small side door, against which was leaning the same kind of ladder-like steps. A tin stovepipe stuck out of the green tarpaper roof. Coupled to it was an even older sagging boxcar. Both were a faded, dirty, chipped mud-red color. I squinted my eyes and tried to imagine a movie set...a mirage that would turn into a honeymoon cottage...but no change. It was still just an ungainly, ragged, tilted, lonely baggage car, with railroad ties for roses.

"What's the matter?" Bill asked.

"Nothing," I stammered. "I just thought...it would be a better color...a little newer looking. It must be a hundred years old!"

He took me in his arms right there in front of the squirrels and Mexicans. "Come in and look at it anyway. You don't have to stay."

We climbed the ladder steps and he pushed open the door. The little glass window in it rattled. Inside, he turned on a light. We had entered a kitchen. In the opposite wall was another door with its little glass window. The room was long, narrow, a shadowy gray. To the right of the other door was a round oilcloth-covered table decorated with a box of cereal, jar of jam, catsup, a glass of toothpicks. Left of the door was a sink and drainboard, unpainted, with cupboards underneath.

"Darned good stove," my husband informed me. "Burns coal. Of course you'll have to get used to it." Anchored at the far left end of the room, it dwarfed everything else. Huge and black, like it had come from some hotel kitchen, it had a massive oven door and a large warming oven. Bill removed two heavy plates and began digging inside with an iron bar, raising a cloud of fine ashes. Just past the stove was another door in the end of the room, sporting a big brass doorknob. The left side of the kitchen was taken up by a kind of tall pantry cupboard and something that looked like a closet.

"This is the shower bath." He pulled aside a burlap curtain, revealing a tin-lined cubicle with faucets, a stool and mirror, some not-too-clean towels. He pointed upward. "The hot water comes from there."

"There isn't any ceiling!" I exclaimed.

"Well, no," he replied, as if I shouldn't have expected one.

Arch after arch of small sections, each with a cobwebbed ventilator, outlined the domed roof. Suspended from the roof, Lord-knows-how, was the "hot water comes from there"; two immense tanks laced with myriads of water pipes that ran down to the stove and to faucets jutting out from the wall over the sink. And finally there was the original bellcord running through the room, now strung with clothes pins.

"See," he said, opening the end door, "you can walk right through here into the tool car. We keep our vegetables in an icebox out there."

"What does the rest look like?" I asked uncertainly.

"Well, the living room is in the middle." He led me in the opposite direction, turning on another overhead light.

On the left side there was sort of a desk in the near corner, against the wall a battered square table with two roundback chairs from some ancient depot. The walls were a dingy cream color, three windows on each side covered by dark green burlap curtains. The floor had worn brown linoleum, and overhead a continuation of the same dusty arched roof.

A pot-bellied iron stove and coal bucket stood on the right, beyond it another chair and a steel cot neatly covered with a blanket and a stand holding some magazines and a pack of cigarettes.

"Thatch sleeps there," Bill said hurriedly. "Now our bedroom is not bad." He went through the living room to a plywood door in a thin partition that didn't reach to the ceiling. He pulled the chain of a pink-shaded bedlamp nailed to the wall. "The bed will be here in place of my cot..."

"Lace curtains!" I cried. Yes, the filmy white dime-store kind were pinned across the two windows. "Bill, did you put them up? Did you buy them?"

"Wanted you to feel at home, Kay-Kay."

I surveyed the small room with its domed roof, high closets across the end wall, a little table with a cracked mirror, a chair and his cot. But dominating the softly lighted chamber were those pathetic lace curtains, tenderly arranged by calloused hands in hopes his wife would be there.

"You poor husband," I smiled. "You poor anxious husband!"

"Think you can stand it?" He waited, watching my face.

I went into his arms, hugging as tightly as I could. "You really love me, don't you? How could I possibly leave you here alone?"

He took the world down off his shoulders — and little did I know — he

5

never intended to pick it up again. I was roped, tied and stowed away in this baggage car in the mountains with a domed ceiling and sixty Mexicans for neighbors.

But he concealed his victory well. He said cheerily, "Well, let's fix a bite to eat and sort of get settled." We went back to the kitchen and its huge cookstove. "Might as well get onto this first," he decided. "You won't have any trouble after you see how it's done."

He lifted off two of the heavy lids, crammed in newspaper, kindling wood, squirted something out of a can and dumped in a generous pile of grimy coal. When he applied a match the arrangement went "woof!".

"Just go easy on the kerosene," he advised. "Now here is the coffee. I'll go down to the car and bring up the rest of our things." He located an electric lantern, kissed me and was gone.

I filled the teakettle, which weighed fifteen pounds with or without water, and proceeded to hunt for dishes. There were plenty in the cupboard, man-size plates and platters, all a half-inch thick, mixed in among cans of tomatoes and sliced peaches. A dozen cups like old shaving mugs hung on nails against the back wall. I lugged two of each to the table and dug out some bread from the box we'd brought. By now the fire was roaring merrily, too merrily. Was I supposed to do something about it? I lifted a lid, smoke and flame flared up. Maybe it would subside by itself...I hoped.

Then, because of the excitement or something, I felt the warning of an impending natural function. Where was the bathroom?

Perhaps in there near the shower...no...maybe in that other car. Chill night air met me when I opened the end door. There was a plank walkway between the cars and another door, but that disclosed only black darkness and smells of coal and creosote. Back in the kitchen the stove was dull red and the kettle boiling wildly. I was ready to holler FIRE when I heard Bill at the side door struggling with the mattress.

"I thought you were going to get help," I reminded him.

Panting, he threw the mattress on the helper's cot. "I made it all right. The rest won't be bad."

I said anxiously, "Dear, where is the..."

"Holy smoke!" He strode to the stove and did something. The roaring subsided. "You've got to turn this damper, Kay. You'll burn the place down!"

"I didn't see that in the instructions."

"Forgot to tell you. What did you want?"

"The bathroom."

"Well, we wash in the sink. Lots of farm people do that. And I showed you the shower."

"You know what I mean."

His face took on a look of despair. "I hoped we wouldn't get to that so soon." He turned on the electric lantern and opened the opposite side door. A forbidding black mountain was out there and a wedge of starlit sky. The light beam picked out a tiny red-painted shack like a telephone booth, nestled between a couple of fir trees.

"You mean that's it?" I cried.

"Shall I go with you the first time?"

"I'm not going! Why, there might be a bear...a wolf...a man..." Men of genius had long ago designed modern plumbing to emancipate people from the backyard privy. Others had created glistening tile bathrooms with warmth and comfort and I was being shown this! I stared at my husband in disbelief.

"Take the lantern," he suggested. "I'll leave this door open for you."

Thinking fondly of my honeymoon cottage and all the friendly bathrooms I'd been in without appreciating them, I crept down the steps and up the dim trail. The flimsy door creaked as I opened it, the lantern beam chased shadows up into the corners. Something bright flashed at me, I almost ran. It was a chromium-plated paper dispenser. The catalog era had gone!

It would be fitting to mention here other forgotten aspects of that little shanty which, I learned, would be forever present and inescapable. Things like the brutal drafts, the night sounds, the utter lack of conducive relaxation, choosing between darkness and the glaring beam of the lantern. Suffice it to say that I did survive the ordeal but not without gaining a new respect for civilization. In commemoration of that first visit I named the place The Dream House". It seemed to lessen the shock.

I hung the lantern back on the big nail where it apparently belonged. Bill had poured fragrant coffee into the thick mugs and made lunchmeat sandwiches. But as we ate there was a strange silence. Then he said, "I know that's the worst part for you, Kay."

"Let's not talk about it," I told him. "People living out in the country have those things. I guess I can put up with it." Then I noticed a rumbling sound like distant thunder. "What's that funny noise?"

"Train coming." He looked at his watch. In fact, any incident involving trains or the railroad automatically brought that gold plated timepiece from his pocket. It had cost seventy-five dollars and taken big bites out of his first paychecks.

I could hear the laboring exhaust of a locomotive approaching with heavy steps, like the tread of a story-book giant. The glass in the door began to vibrate quietly, then frantically. The knives and forks joined in, my chair quivering with them. The noise became a roar that thundered through the

7

walls in a gushing torrent.

"Are they all like this?" I cried. "The noise is terrible!"

He nodded. Apparently you abandoned all conversation when a train was coming. The crashing blasts came closer, louder, until my eardrums ached. A shot jarred in the room. I leaped to my feet wild-eyed.

Bill laughed and caught my arm. "Oven door fell open," he hollered in my ear. "Have to fix it sometime. Like to watch the engine go by?"

He opened the side door and less than fifteen feet away the curving rails were steely white in the blinding glare of an approaching headlight. The roar shook the very marrow of my bones as the headlight crept abreast of us with the cab seemingly an arm's length away and the engineer silhouetted by shaded lamps, followed by the ponderous, thrashing machinery of the engine.

"Cab-in-front Mallet," Bill shouted. "Espee is the only one that has this kind."

A column of black smoke blotted out the stars. The hulking shape of the tender loomed, following the stomping beat of its leader. Then a boxcar trundled past, strangely big in the light from our doorway, and another, still another, wheels screaming against the curve. The pounding of the engine receded to give us back some of our hearing. Bill said, "Want to come in now?"

"Can we watch it all go by?" Something unexplainable held me fascinated; the rumbling march of the cars as they appeared and disappeared like ghosts. Some rattled along, some trod smoothly, others screeched in protest, all keeping the same measured pace. They brought unexpected odors; the smell of apples, the fragrance of new lumber, oil.

"Mixed train," Bill said. "Little of everything in its consist. It's called a 'drag'."

I had the feeling I was watching the pulsating life-blood of modern existence, exciting, vital, unpraised. When I thought the end must surely be near I heard more engine sounds. "Is there another engine?" I exclaimed.

He nodded. "All trains have helpers over these mountains."

"Not again!" I pushed inside and slammed the door.

Yes, again. The glass in the door was already vibrating. The frightening crescendo had started over again, roaring through the room without mercy. I thought, how many times has this old baggage car withstood these poundings? How many times would I be able to stand them? And hardly had the engine receded when I could hear another!

"Three engines on one train?" I questioned.

Bill nodded. He was calmly finishing the last of the coffee.

I thought, surely he must be suffering a little. He must be! There was a sudden sound like a shot; the oven door fell open again.

I lay in bed with the blanket up under my chin, watching the shadows on the domed ceiling as my husband undressed. He clumped his shoes into a corner, hung up overalls and shirt. Then he sat on the edge of the bed and checked the alarm clock with his watch. "Cooler up here, huh?"

He slid into bed. "Glad to be with your husband again?"

I felt his warmth and the coziness of our bed, or was it the lace curtains, or the quiet night outside? Something began to brush away the loneliness of the past weeks. I was still not sure that I wasn't a little balmy to get myself into such a weird place, the south end of a baggage car parked in some forgotten mountains. But the loneliness was gone. This Sunday night I'd be with him instead of sleeping alone miles away.

"You'll like it up here, Kay," Bill promised. "The clear air and scenery are wonderful. Once you get used to it you'll see the importance and romance of railroading."

"I haven't made up my mind to stay yet."

He put out the light and pulled me to him. "Then I'll have to convince you!" He kissed me in exaggerated movie star style and took a long time about it. He felt the satisfaction sweep through my veins and waited for me to bring the kiss to an end. "Now how was that?" he teased.

"I'd have sworn it must be Clark Gable."

He laughed and kissed me again, turning to bring us closer, to push my fears away and carry me into the realm of honeymooners. I forgot about Clark Gable and remembered the lace curtains and how necessary husbands are. Being completely together like this was the most important part, to drift away and not think about time or things, just think about us.

Then I felt the cool air as he drew the blanket up around my shoulders and lay there holding my hand. Out in the night a train whistle sounded, long and lonesome.

"They sound romantic at night," I admitted.

He squeezed my hand. Far off there was a dull rumbling sound. The whistle sounded again, closer. Two long blasts, a short, a long.

"He's coming downgrade," Bill said.

The rumbling grew louder, joined by the clatter of the locomotive as a light flashed across the curtains. The engine charged past, followed by a jarring clackety-clacking parade of boxcars. I gripped my husband's arm against the quivering mattress. Then I sat up suddenly.

"Bill, I smell something burning."

"It's from the train," he explained. "Hot brakes."

I lay back in the darkness and listened to the racket outside, the trembling old baggage car, the acrid odor of hot wheels in the bedroom, and wondered how anyone could sleep in such a bedlam. Bill had turned over before the last car went clattering away in the night.

Suddenly I sat bolt upright again. Light was leaking over the thin partition. Heavy footsteps. "Bill," I whispered, "someone's in the other room!"

"Must be Thatch coming in," he grunted.

I slumped back stealthily, listening to the squeaks of the steel cot. Clump, clump — he was taking off his shoes. Clink, clink — some change tossed onto the bedside stand. The jingle of a belt buckle as he removed trousers turned me cold and tense. I felt for the safety of Bill's arm.

"Relax," my husband mumbled.

"What if he'd come in a few minutes ago? While we were . . . making love."

Bill rolled over to face me. He whispered, "Look, you don't have to worry about Thatch. He's okay."

The guy practically walks in on our love scene and my husband says, 'He's okay'! My heart sank. How could he ignore another man a few feet away? The cot squeaked with each turn the intruder made and each squeak poured ice into my veins.

Wide awake I listened to my husband's breathing and wondered about men. What code of ethics did they have for this situation? What terse understanding before I came? I pictured Bill discussing me with his helper before I arrived and the ice clinked in my frightened arteries. That brought on the unexpected but demanding urge so common to women. I nudged him. "Bill?" I whispered.

"Huh?"

"I have to go."

He turned over. "Well, go ahead then."

"I can't traipse through that room with him there in bed."

"Oh, for gosh sake." I could feel him thinking over the problem. "Can't talk yourself out of it?" he asked softly.

"Of course not! You'll have to do something."

With a sigh he rolled out of bed, got the flashlight, and went shuffling off in his slippers. In a minute he was back, but he stopped at the door and said, "Hi, Thatch."

"Hiya," a low voice answered. "Wife come up?"

"Yeah."

"Good deal."

Bill pulled shut the thin door. The flashlight shone on a bright red two-pound coffee can. "Here," he offered. "Best I could do." He put the flashlight in my hand and piled into bed.

I thought about all the people in the world who had green-tiled bathrooms

An eastbound passenger train of the 1940 era takes on water before tackling the climb to Donner Summit.   *(Walter Keck collection)*

and didn't appreciate them, but I could not bring myself to get up in the darkness with a stranger listening.

Bill mumbled, "What are you waiting for?"

"For him to go to sleep."

It took a little while but eventually kindness overcame his impatience. Flashlight on clock, he suggested, "Number Twenty-eight, passenger train should go by in about ten minutes. Will that help?"

It would be a godsend if I could hold out that long. I waited. No Number 28. I nudged Bill.

His steady breathing halted. "Train must be late."

"How much late do you suppose?"

"Ask the company, don't ask me."

It was a tortuous fifteen minutes before I finally heard engine sounds approaching. When it roared past I jumped out of bed as flashes of light from the Pullmans flickered across our curtains. I wondered frantically if the train would be long enough.

Thank God it was and, with the Overland Limited clicking away into the night, I crept back into bed feeling like a chilled, neglected kitten.

I was awakened first by another freight train plodding up the mountain. It advanced with ponderous steps that became a terrifying crash of noise, shaking the bed as it roared through the room. At the instant of being too great to endure the roar receded to be replaced by the march of countless squealing boxcars. The climax of two helper engines came blasting by, stomped me into insensibility, and went on. Bill only stirred in his sleep.

An hour later two 'down' trains passed. I condescendingly awoke for them, smelled their hot brakes, and bid them goodbye. I wondered how Bill could sleep so soundly, and Thatch beyond the partition, the other men in these weird camp cars.

Then there was a lull, as if people had quit shipping things or going anywhere. Determinedly, I tried again and must have slept for two hours. Half dreaming, I suddenly sensed a bright flash of light. An explosion of crashing sound hit me, rocking the whole room.

"Bill!" I sat up in bed and threw my arms around my husband. From the racing clickclackclickclack I realized it must be some new, diabolical kind of train. I cried, "Bill, what is it?"

"For gosh sake," he grumbled. Flashlight on the clock, he explained, "That's the night mail train."

"Do they have to go so fast?" I moaned.

"You'll get used to them, Kay-Kay."

"Did you sit up in bed at first?"

"I guess so." Fully awake now, he held me tightly. He explained there was a Second 88 and another passenger train to go by before daylight, and probably some freights. "Don't be frightened. Hold my hand and try to sleep."

They didn't catch me napping again. I heard the next one blasting up the mountain toward us. This must be Second 88 and from its speed I guessed the engineer was racing to catch his brother on First 88. I could picture him standing up in the swaying cab, holding the throttle wide open. The room, the bed and the lace curtains shook violently as the huge locomotive charged past at our very feet, followed by the frantic clickclackclickclack of wheels. Lights from the coaches flickered across the curtains and rushed off into the night, engine echoes fading among the mountains. Except for Bill's steady breathing, the room was still again.

Dear husband, I prayed, isn't this a little too much? Sleeping in a decrepit railroad car ... a bedlam of racing trains ... sharing our privacy with a stranger ... coal stoves ... outdoor privies? Was it all actually real?

I pictured our little honeymoon cottage with its rose garden on two sides and the past months of a loving marriage. Why had we left it behind? Because of a darkening cloud of temporary jobs and no money. I thought about Dad Letterman, how he had encouraged Bill to get on the railroad, no matter if the first years would be hard going. And before that, when he had convinced us both not to wait, to go ahead and get married.

And before that — a whole year before — when I first saw Bill, in a neat gray suit, getting out of his beautiful blue sport roadster with a mirror on each fender, nickel-plated covers over the yellow wire wheels in each fender well, and rich leather seats. My first ride with him that sunny day, our first kiss...

2. A Canary And Twenty Dollars

Vicki was on the telephone when the blue sports roadster pulled up at the curb in front of the typewriter shop. The top was down. A handsome young fellow in a neat gray suit got out and came around to the curb side. He was fairly tall, thinning brown hair, maybe twenty-four. He took a large typewriter from the seat and came toward the shop, carrying it in front of him.

"Vicki, who is that?" I asked.

"Oh, it's Bill Fisher, our salesman." She covered the phone. "Open the door, will you Kay."

I rushed to help him. He halted in the doorway, holding the heavy machine. He had dark green eyes and a mischievous smile.

"Well, hello goodlooking. Who are you?" he asked.

"I'm Kay, Vicki's cousin." I let him look me over.

He rested the typewriter on a counter among the new ones. "Vicki, you've been holding out on me! You didn't tell me you had a cute cousin like Kay."

Vicki stammered, "I guess you two just didn't happen to be in the store at the same time. Bill, meet my cousin . . ."

"We have just met," he broke in, grinning at me. "I'll take this monster to the mechanic out back, and then we'll talk about it. I didn't make a sale but I left the other machine as a loaner and got this repair job anyway. Kay, don't you go away!" He grasped the machine, taking care that his blue tie didn't get into the type. "Darned legal size machines are heavy."

Vicki said, "Isn't he handsome? And he's single, Kay!"

"He sure is goodlooking," I agreed. "Kind of slender, though. Why haven't I seen him before?" My rooming house was only a few blocks away so I often walked up to visit Vicki when I was not working. Jobs were so hard to find. I'd do typing when I could get it, housework, waitress work now and then, but I hated that.

"My brother won't pay Bill a salary, only straight commission, so he stops in when he thinks he might have a sale. I think he's involved in some small printing business, too."

Bill came back and handed Vicki a paper. "Here's the firm name, kid. That office manager will faint when you tell him it's fifteen bucks. Ask that brother of yours what he'll offer on a trade-in. Maybe I still can make a sale."

Vicki gave him a dollar and a half commission.

"Man, I can eat for a week on that," he kidded her. "But let's get back to your cousin. Kay, you two gals both have dark brown eyes and black hair. How come?"

"We're Syrian descent," I told him. Vicki was short with a perfect figure. I was medium height but too wide in back and too large in front. Bill didn't seem to mind.

"Bet you're warm blooded, huh?" He ignored my blush. "I've been trying to entice Vicki for weeks but she says she's engaged to some Joe guy in L.A. I don't believe her."

"Kay," Vicki put in, "don't pay attention to that line of his!"

"I love your car," I said. "It looks racy."

"It's a 1929 Chrysler," he smiled. "Gets me lots of looks from the gals when I drive down the street. Getting a little old, though. Want to take a ride? I've got a couple of more calls. Come on, I'm harmless."

We drove down the busy street in the warm May sunshine. When Bill had to stop for streetcars or traffic we attracted admiring glances. The car had rich leather upholstery and plate glass windwings, a jaunty winged radiator cap, and a rumble seat. He headed out of town on U.S. 40, the wind swirling my hair. The romance of spring was in the air. I was in seventh heaven.

"Hey, you're pretty with your hair mussed," he teased. He swung off at the Dreamland Ballroom. "I'm trying to get a poster order from this guy for their next dance. Come on in with me."

The empty dance hall looked huge. While he went into the office I strolled over the polished spring floor, wondering if I'd be dancing here with Bill some night to the music of Harry James or Rudy Vallee.

"Well," he announced, going back to the Chrysler, "I got an order for a thousand but he sure argued me down in price."

We drove back into town, stopping at a paper warehouse where he placed an order for poster stock, and then to my rooming house. At the curb, he said, "Sure is a nice old place, good neighborhood. Got a phone?"

"A pay phone at the end of the hall."

He squeezed my hand against the leather seat. "I'll see you again soon. Maybe tomorrow."

I sailed up the stone steps and down the hall to "Ma" Fitzgerald's apartment. She owned the rooming house and was about the only mother I had. Her husband, a railroad engineer, had passed away and this was her livelihood. She was a large woman, with the warmth and down-to-earth nature of Kansas heritage. She was ironing sheets in the kitchen as she listened to my bubbling description of Bill and his car and our day.

"I'd just guess, Kay." She folded up the sheet. "But lookin' at the wind, I'd say you were in love!"

I suppose that was the beginning. Wrapped in a hopechest of dreams I had no premonition of struggles ahead, marriage, or the completely impossible thought of sleeping in a railroad car in the mountains.

We did dance together at Dreamland whenever we could muster the admission, once to Rudy Vallee's orchestra which cost extra. Bill kissed me under the dim lights as we glided to soft music, and being in love seemed to be the only thing that kept us going against the continual hassle of temporary jobs and little money.

I rode with him often in the Chrysler as he made his 'calls'. Sometimes it was trying to sell poster orders for dances, football games, races, or pounding the pavement to make a typewriter sale. Selling jobs were plentiful but none paid a salary; he'd found that selling on straight commission was the starvation route. He had his name in several all-night restaurants and got in a few shifts when some employee was sick. Most of all he wanted to make the poster business succeed; it was a chance to beat the job hunting.

He and a tall young friend, Bob, who was a good artist, had a shop in a small building on the edge of town. Bob was married and worked part-time for an advertising agency. Between them they'd silk-screen advertising posters when Bill could get orders. Bob did the stencil cutting. They had named their business Trueprint Poster Service. Often we'd have a 'date' at the shop where I'd rack the wet placards as they printed them.

On warm summer evenings Bill would take me home the long way; out along the river highway where we could park under the trees.

Vicki sometimes found a few days typing work for me, and I accepted housework calls through Ma Fitzgerald's phone number, but learned that most

Kay and the good old Chrysler.

of the women who called wanted you to clean their whole house without stopping, for 15¢ an hour. I took waitress jobs when there was nothing else, for tips and meals only, no wages. Bill and I would have a "date" when either of us had enough for some gas, a cup of coffee and a breakfast roll divided in two.

The good old Chrysler was our ship in a storm. One hot afternoon in September we decided to forget about the world and go on a picnic. A sack of eats from a delicatessen and a few miles up the river route put us in a world of cool breezes, birds in the trees, and privacy. Bill enjoyed the tasty lunch. He was leaning on one elbow, smiling at me.

"Say, goodlooking, how about you and I getting married?"

The sun beamed down on us, the birds turned up their volume, my pulse doubled. "I accept on one condition," I announced between the first and second kiss. "That you kiss me every morning and every night!"

"And every chance between times," he promised, with appropriate hugs and kisses. "At least we'd have to pay only one room rent instead of two."

"But when?" I asked – and the world of no jobs, money, and struggle for security rose up beyond the trees and birds.

"If the poster business improves," Bill suggested. "Maybe by the first of the year."

We had a lot in common. We were both twenty-five and both poor. Both of

16

us had been badly trampled by the Depression.

My parents had died in the flu epidemic of the '20s, leaving two brothers and me orphans. In my later grade school years we lived in orphanages or sometimes with relatives. Through high school we were wards of the County in our home state in the middle west. Our father had had a business in a small town in the wheat country and that was held in trust to support us. We'd reached our late teens when the hard times and dust storms lay over the country. With little money coming from the trust, my brothers decided we should come to Sacramento. An aunt and uncle had a grocery store and would provide jobs for the boys. I came along as their housekeeper. Then early last year, 1939, with times improving in the Dakotas, my brothers chose to go back home and try to open our father's business again. I hated the thought of those forty-below-zero winters and snow, so I chose to stay. I may have been hoping a husband would appear!

Bill finished high school in 1929 in the Northwest, moved south to start a college course in electrical engineering – and collided with the first wave of the Depression. He'd also lost his mother in the second year of high school, and had only a sister living in a foothill town. Instead of college, he attended, as he put it, the School of Hard Knocks.

After a year or so of farm work at a dollar a day when he could get it, he'd headed for the hills. Prospecting, mining, even woodcutting, restaurant work, part-time jobs wiring houses for a contractor kept him reading the Help Wanted. When Roosevelt initiated the NRA program, Bill decided the city might offer more opportunity. He'd traded his Star truck in on the Chrysler at a used car lot.

"She's beginning to use oil," he warned, as we drove back toward town.

"I don't care! I'm so happy I could float on Cloud Nine."

Ma Fitzgerald hugged me when I gushed out the news I was engaged. She did not ask about a ring, or our plans for a wedding date.

Aunt Rosalie invited us for dinner. I knew she just wanted to look Bill over but he agreed to go; it was about the only 'family' I had. Uncle Morse shook Bill's hand but didn't offer him a job. After dinner, doing dishes in the kitchen, Aunty whispered, "Kay, if he doesn't have a steady job, didn't even give you a ring . . ."

"Don't worry," I said. "That doesn't bother me a bit."

Aunty had four children and they had weathered the Depression all right, but I wasn't sure if she was happily married or not. As we were leaving, little Carol, five, asked, "Aunt Kay-Kay, can I come to your wedding?" To her I seemed too old to be a cousin.

"Of course, but you'll have to wait. We don't know when it will be yet."

Bill put in, "Hey, I like that name, Kay-Kay. I'll call you that."

So I became Kay-Kay when he was feeling affectionate, but otherwise I was still 'Kay'.

It rained in October. I had to sit close to him in the car because the top leaked on my side, but the side curtains kept out the wind. Bill made a good typewriter sale so we treated ourselves to a Harry James dance. We waltzed so perfectly, oblivious to everyone else. Love was wonderful!

But on the first of November poor paper stock caused a large order of football posters to curl up like autumn leaves. Our Saturday night date was spent at the shop rushing through a new order, knowing the profit and then some was gone. The business weathered the storm in a staggering sort of way.

By December things looked hopeful and we talked about Christmas. The first of the year was only weeks away.

Then the sheriff closed a gala new nightclub on opening night and the Trueprint Poster Service received a body blow. Fifteen hundred posters in three-color didn't get paid for. The little company was broke.

"I don't mind waiting to get married," I told him. The Chrysler was parked in the pouring rain under a street light in front of my rooming house.

He held me tightly. "Kay-Kay, I can't ask you to wait indefinitely. We might never get the business going again."

"June weddings are nice," I suggested.

"That's so far away. Let's try for April."

He kissed me at the front door. I climbed the steps to my room thinking about our picnic in the grass and his proposal, Aunty's objections, Ma Fitzgerald's quiet encouragement. I didn't sleep very well that night.

A week later I got on as an extra clerk in a department store at 25¢ an hour. Bill, too, got on as a waiter in an all-night cafe; twelve dollars a week and two meals. So he phoned when he could, but we had few dates. We both knew that the temporary jobs would provide a few dollars but we'd be laid off a day or two before Christmas.

Christmas Eve was cold and foggy but no rain so we walked along the main streets in the evening admiring the elaborate displays in store windows. We agreed there was no point in exchanging gifts. The one thing I wanted was an engagement ring, and Bill wanted to make a down payment on one, but I insisted we save what money we had. Aunty had invited us for dinner Christmas Day but I said we had other plans. I didn't say we couldn't afford gifts for the kids. We had coffee in a cafe, splurged on a piece of pie, and agreed that tomorrow we'd just go for a ride in the country.

Chilly air but a bright sun made it pleasant cruising along the nearly deserted highway. "Oh, turn off here," I said suddenly, "I know some retired people who have a farm." Watching the mail boxes, "There, Letterman, turn there." I'd been here with Ma Fitzgerald several times, coming on the bus from town. Mr. Letterman had worked in the railroad shops so they and Ma and her husband had been friends for years.

Like an oasis in the drab fields, the Spanish-style house was an artist's picture shaded by huge oak trees and surrounded by scores of prize rose bushes, a primrose covered tank house, an arbor supporting colorful gourd vines, and smoke drifting from the fireplace.

Tillie Letterman didn't look like a grandmother as she came out to greet us. A little on the heavy side, her figure had suffered from raising a big family, taking off and putting on weight, but you didn't see that or the gray hair because her eyes twinkled with a zest for living.

"Kay, what a nice surprise to see you! I guess this is Bill." She offered a handshake. "Kay, I talked to Ma on the phone this morning and she told me about your plans to get married. I'm so happy for you two."

We stood bewildered at the quick hospitality, her attitude that we were virtually family to her.

"Come on in," she insisted. "Dad is still in his slippers and robe but I made him put on some trousers."

Dad Letterman, slender with white hair and almost boyish face in spite of his seventy years, reached for Bill's hand, peering over his glasses. "Young feller, I'm happy to meet you. You've got a real fine gal here. We know more about her than she thinks."

The room was old and homey, with the feeling of being lived in. Dad stirred the fire while Tillie puttered around getting some fruit cake and a glass of red wine for everyone. Dad carefully lighted his pipe, holding it in his hand while he smoked because of his false teeth and leaned back in his easy chair.

"Gettin' married is a big event for young people," he declared. "Have you set a date?"

"No sir, we haven't," Bill replied, very embarrassed. "We are kind of planning on April."

"Too long. You both might change your mind by then." He drew on his pipe, looking at us over the glasses. "Tillie and me been married fifty-one years. I was a young buck pitchin' hay for her father and Tillie was only sixteen. When I proposed to her the old man run me off the place! We went off and got married. If we'd waited, we never would have made it. We've never been sorry, have we darlin'?"

Neither Bill nor I could think of anything to say.

"My, that was a long time ago, Kay," Tillie said. "I'm so glad you two came out; it makes me remember our blessings. Yes, we settled right here on

19

this piece of ground, built a barn with our own hands, and lived in one end, with two cows and some chickens in the rest. Dad worked for the neighbors to make ends meet. You two are old enough to know what you are doing."

"Did pretty good with the cows and hiring out," Dad remembered. "But I didn't like farming. When them new-fangled Ford cars came out we bought one and I went in town and rustled a job in the Espee shops. Tillie wanted to stay in the country so I drove the seven miles every day. I guess I was the first commuter."

Tillie replenished the fruit cake and wine, Dad refilled his pipe. "Now why do you two want to wait 'til April?" he wanted to know.

Money, Bill explained. He told Dad about the troubles of the Trueprint Poster Service and job hunting. I realized that Bill had the world on his shoulders; he was seriously in love with me and knew we should be married.

"I know you have to eat," Dad said, "and meet the bills. If this here printing thing don't work out you'll have to get a steady job. And I know that isn't easy nowadays. But that's not the important thing."

We respected his advice, this man who'd been married to the same girl so long, had worked 40 years in the railroad shops and worn out ten Fords. But what could be more important than having enough money?

"Sickness comes along," Dad said abruptly. "Hardship, another man or another woman, times when you'll be wonderin' if you did the right thing. Then is when you'll find out money isn't the most important."

"What is the important thing then, Mr. Letterman?" Bill wondered.

"Once you start out, you got to make up your mind to stayin' together no matter what happens. Make up your mind to stayin' married."

All that was in the vows, we felt. For better or worse . . . in sickness and health. That part seemed to be a foregone conclusion. Perhaps Dad couldn't see our side, now that he was a retired gentleman farmer with a nice home and a new car in the driveway. But later on I was to remember his words many times.

"First thing you folks need is a place to live, to set up housekeeping," Dad stated. "Now Tillie and me have a cottage on the back slope. Started it as a two-car garage couple of years ago. Then a grandson was planning to get married so we remodeled it into a house. The kids didn't hit it off and the place never got used. Why don't we go out and have a look at it? Darlin', you mind gettin' me a shirt?"

Bundled against the chill air, they led us across the damp lawn and around the rose garden. The little building was finished in pink stucco, with two large windows in front, and a cute front porch. Inside it was divided into a narrow bedroom and small living room, both lined with new knotty pine. Dad had

Organ music, relatives, but no cake.

added a section to the rear to form a sunny little kitchen and a bathroom. I could picture a confusion of roses and flowers around the outside when spring came. It was a perfect honeymoon cottage.

"We'll rent it to you for fifteen dollars a month," Dad offered, "with the first month free."

Fifteen dollars and the first month free!

We drove back to town in a Chrysler equipped with dove-like wings. We'd told Tillie and Dad we'd let them know within a week.

In that week Dad reminded us he had more to do on the cupboards and we'd better make it two weeks — if we could stand it that long. It hadn't occurred to us we'd need some furniture, but it had to Mrs. Letterman. She gave us a walnut bedstead and mattress, a used rug for the living room, a table and four unmatched chairs, some throw rugs. I had some towels and linens left from housekeeping for my brothers, Bill had a few pots and pans from his batching years, Ma Fitzgerald gave us four sheets, two quilts and an electric iron.

The little cottage looked darling. The Lettermans were happy for us. We had twenty dollars, all that was left in the accounts of the Trueprint Poster Service.

So on a sunny afternoon two weeks after New Year's and two weeks before the car license was due, we got married. The ceremony was performed in a little church in the town where Bill's sister lived, complete with organ music, flowers, and relatives, but no cake.

"If I ever get married again," I told my new husband, "I want a cake."

"Kay-Kay, if you ever get married again I'll break your neck."

Love was wonderful!

When we arrived back at the cottage there was a note on the door.

"Dear Kay and Bill; We have gone on a two weeks vacation trip. Hope everything is O.K. Your wedding present is inside. His name is Bucky. Dad and Tillie."

We opened the door and there, placed on an apple box, was a shiny new birdcage containing a sad looking canary. He said, "Peep."

"That," Bill observed, "is just what we need. A canary."

"I guess Tillie thought it would make our house cheery." I didn't know what else to say. "But, husband dear, you didn't carry me over the threshold."

We went back outside and he duly carried me inside. The house smelled clean and cozy, and I loved it. I even liked Bucky.

"Wonder why the folks took a trip this time of year," Bill mused.

"We are newlyweds, remember?"

"What difference does that make?"

He was serious, so help me! I was to live and learn about husbands.

3. The Wheels Turn

Even that first month when we couldn't have paid the rent, or the second when we didn't, I worried not one bit. Bill was doing enough worrying for both of us.

It wasn't hard to read the Trueprint Poster Service's balance sheet, and we'd learned there are certain fixed expenses in being married even if you don't eat. We still had some of the twenty dollars we started out with, but we didn't have much. Winter weather had slowed the poster orders to almost none. We had two dollars, and were down to beans.

"Dad has been after me to go to work for the railroad," Bill told me. "Think I should?"

"Whatever you think best. I still have faith in the poster business." I stood close to him so he would automatically take me in his arms. But I began to think a little more about Dad's words: You've got to make up your mind to staying married.

Bill came home from the railroad shops with a timely light on the transportation business. "The railroad is having a slack season, too," he said dejectedly. "Nothing before April or May."

"You'll get some poster orders this week, I'm sure."

"I'm glad you're sure. I'm not. Have you got any money left? The Chrysler is out of gas."

"Two dollars, but we're out of food."

"We'll split it. One dollar for food, one for gas."

As it turned out his half brought the biggest returns. He came home that evening with four gallons still in the tank and a big grin on his face. "Kay-Kay, the Trueprint Poster Service is in the lumber business!"

"Lumber business? Without any money?"

"We both got jobs today piling lumber, part-time."

So my husband became a working man two or three days a week. When there was no lumber to pile he would don suit and tie and become a poster salesman. During February and March we had a little trouble with the wolf outside the door. It rained hard. The top of the car got to leaking worse.

In the meantime, my Aunt had pointed out that things were turning out just as she expected. "A person just can't get along without money, Kay," she said. "I don't know what you are going to do."

"She could help," Bill commented, "by minding her own potatoes."

These and other storm warnings did not escape the watchful eye of Dad Letterman. He matter-of-factly asked Bill what progress he'd made in getting on the railroad, and suggested we not worry about the rent. In spite of slack times Dad was doing things to get the slow-moving wheels of corporation turning in our favor. But we didn't know so we went right on living on love, with time out now and then to give the wolf a good kick.

It was a cold, cloudy Sunday. Bill was in the backyard working on the Chrysler, grinding the valves, which he said were in very bad shape. I went out there with another problem.

"Bill, the Lettermans are having company and I'm afraid she is going to bring them over to see us. They are out in the yard."

"Well, I hope not, because I'd like to get this done before it rains." He went on furiously cranking the valve grinding tool.

"Well, I hope not, because we don't have any furniture."

He stopped cranking, looked at the parts scattered around and up at the threatening sky. "Kay, I'm sorry we don't have any furniture, or a better car, or money enough to have friends over for dinner."

"Bill Fisher, don't you say things like that!"

"That's the way I feel."

"Well, don't feel like that. If they want to come and see our house, well let them. They look like very nice people."

"Holy smoke, it's beginning to rain." A few drops had fallen, leaving wet spots on the car. He hurried to get the last valves done while I tried to help by handing him tools. Suddenly we looked up to find Dad and another man standing there.

"Think you'll ever get her together?" Dad asked. He was dressed in his Sunday suit, grinning at the surprise he'd given us. The other man was portly, smooth-faced. He wore a severe blue suit and a hat set very straight on his head.

"Always been able to finish anything I started," Bill answered. "Got a good helper today, too."

The man smiled appreciatively. Dad said, "Kids, this is Mr. Leech. He's division engineer down at the company."

Bill struggled to wipe the grease from his hands. We knew immediately that 'the company' was the Southern Pacific. Rain began to fall in persistent little drops as they shook hands.

"More parts to these things than a locomotive," Mr. Leech observed. Careful not to get close to the grease, he listened with interest as Bill explained what he was doing. "I'm sure many of us would be better drivers if we knew as much about our automobiles. The folks tell me you are interested in working for the railroad."

"Yes sir," Bill replied. "Haven't had much luck so far."

"Bad time of year. What type of work do you do?"

Bill grasped for something that would fit railroads, and realized he didn't know what railroad men do beside run trains. "I've done mechanical work, wiring."

"Wiring?"

"House wiring, electric motors, things like that."

"Hm. Well, keep trying." He turned away. The rain drops plunked on the fenders of the Chrysler. The surprise and lack of success left us staring at each other.

I said, "For goodness sake, he didn't offer much encouragement." It was a meager incentive; keep trying. Bill had to cover the motor with a canvas and finish the job the next day. The little house looked rather insecure that night. "Maybe you should see Mr. Leech at his office," I suggested. "When you get the car running."

We asked Dad Letterman what he thought. No good, Dad said. Better not bother him for a while. Railroad officials — 'brass hats' he called them — were that way. They never hurried, never said anything. "Leech liked you folks, though."

"Just what does the division engineer do?" we asked.

"Well, he's the chief brass hat of the Maintenance of Way," Dad explained. "That's everything outside of Operating, which is the business of running trains. He has charge of all the track, bridges, signals, tunnels, buildings and that stuff."

In March Bill got on as a counterman in an all-night cafeteria and we were able to pay February's rent. He had to take a shift from ten p.m. to six in the morning so I had to sleep alone, while he slept from seven to about three in the afternoon. It wasn't the best arrangement for newlyweds but it kept the wolf from the door. I couldn't listen to my favorite daytime radio programs. We were able to buy a chest of drawers secondhand for $3.00 and a library table for the living room.

As April came along with warm spring rains and some sunny days our little honeymoon cottage became surrounded with a profusion of flowers and blossoming roses; Tillie had scores of prize Cecil Breuners. Bees and humming birds appeared. I loved my little house.

This morning I was outside puttering in the rose garden so as not to disturb Bill when Tillie came hurrying out of her house. "Kay, Mr. Leech's office is on the phone. They want to talk to Bill."

"Oh, my goodness, he's asleep. Do you think I should answer? They might hang up before I can get him to the phone."

The girl on the line was very efficient. "Please hold on, Mrs. Fisher . . ." Then Mr. Leech's voice, "Good morning, Mrs. Fisher, and how are you?"

"We are both fine," I stammered. "I'm sorry we were so busy the day you were here. We . . ."

"Well, it was a rather rainy day, but we enjoyed meeting you. Tell me, is your husband still interested in working for the Southern Pacific?"

"Oh, yes, Mr. Leech! He isn't here right now but I know he is. Shall I call him to the phone?"

"That's not necessary. Just tell him, if he's interested, to come in to our offices about seven-thirty tomorrow. Have him stop at the gate and get directions to the Stores Department. Goodbye, and give my regards to the Lettermans."

Of course I was on pins and needles until Bill woke up. He didn't seem too surprised; he suspected that Dad had been helping in the background. At dinner he decided he'd work his night shift at the restaurant and then go to the S.P. offices in the morning.

"I don't think they pay any more than I'm making now," he said. "Less, considering the two meals I get, probably. But the main thing is it's steady and there's a chance to work up."

It was after three the next afternoon when he finally got home, completely bushed from lack of sleep. "It took all morning to fill out the papers," he reported, "and then I had to take a physical examination. The doc noticed I was tired and he asked me how long I'd been married!" Bill hugged me affectionately and kissed me on the ear. "I just let him think what he wanted to."

While he showered I got a good dinner on the table, and then he filled in the details. The wages were forty cents an hour, they paid only twice a month. "Amazing complex of yards and buildings," he went on. "I had no idea there was so much to railroads. The Stores Department handles everything from nuts and bolts, bits and pieces, to telegraph poles, barrels of oil, switches, rails, ties. I'll be in the track material section. I sort of gathered you have to start at the bottom."

It was nearly five o'clock the next day when the Chrysler pulled into the yard, but he didn't come bouncing in full of enthusiasm. He pulled off his jacket and collapsed in a chair. "I sure learned one thing, Kay-Kay. Everything around a railroad is heavy! I stacked angle bars all day, the things for connecting rails together. They weigh about sixty pounds apiece."

For the next three weeks he came home talking about heel blocks, gauge plates, frogs — which weren't little green things that jumped — but massive rail sections used in switches. But he toughened into the work while I worried about our money running out while we waited for payday.

When he finally brought home the first check, a long green paper with important signatures, we both admired it. "Bill, isn't it wonderful! Thirty-seven dollars and ninety cents."

"They took out fifty cents for hospitalization."

"The first time! That isn't fair."

But we were able to pay the overdue rent for March, buy a recapped tire and some work gloves, and juggle the budget enough to splurge on two steaks for dinner. The steaks were a real extravagance; they cost 53¢ for two.

And in the following weeks we quickly got the payday habit. The first investments were a secondhand overstuffed chair and sofa, another tire. I was still short of dishes and we needed a refrigerator as the first warm days of May arrived, but other things made up for these. It was easy to be in love in our cozy little house in the midst of Tillie's lush flower garden. "The only thing wrong with this place is that dumb canary," Bill complained one day. "Why doesn't he sing?"

"I don't know but I like Bucky anyway. He is a wedding present, remember."

Bill hadn't liked him, nor the name, and didn't see why a canary should need a name. He whistled, threatened, and finally defied the poor thing to give forth one warbling note. "He can't sing," Bill declared. "He's mute."

But one morning I had "Sally's Other Husband" on the radio and was outside among the flowers. The radio got too loud and I thought I should go in and turn it down. Suddenly Bucky began to sing. His vibrant notes came out clear and lusty above the booming voices, and when the organ theme came on he really cut loose. When I went inside he was fairly bursting his lungs trying to outdo the radio. But the din was terrific, I had to turn it down. And then he stopped.

"Bucky, that was wonderful!" I told him. "Won't you sing with the radio just medium?" No, he wouldn't. Not until I turned up the volume, and then he came in like Caruso.

I told Bill about it when he came home, so he experimented. Bucky was very cooperative, turning himself on as soon as the racket reached an impossible level. He wasn't fussy, any program would do just so it was loud! "Silliest thing I ever heard of," Bill said.

"Maybe he's deaf," I suggested.

"Deaf, my foot. He's just stubborn. "

Whichever it was, the little bird would not give in, nor would Bill try to like him. So we reached a deadlock on the subject of Bucky.

One thing, however, of much greater importance, began to cast a shadow over our little house. Bill didn't like his job. He said it was monotonous, hot, heavy work with little prospect of improving. It hardly seemed like railroading; he never even saw any of the trains. "But don't worry about it," he assured me. "I'm not going to quit until I run across something better."

I need not have worried. The great complex wheels of the railroad were turning and our future was getting thoroughly mixed up in the process. He sailed into the driveway one evening, full of news.

"Guess what, I got transferred today!" He kissed me soundly on the ear. "Signal Department. The supervisor, Mr. Browning said Leech's office recommended me because my experience sounded 'diversified'. I go to work in Roseville tomorrow in a signal repair gang."

I was thrilled at his enthusiasm. "Are signals those things with arms, along the tracks?"

"Yeh, block signals. They control all the operation of the trains. They're electrical. I'll be right out there on the line, more like railroading. And it pays a nickel an hour more."

If I had any illusions of him driving home triumphantly the next day like a determined husband who had finally found his purpose in life, I was disillusioned when the time came.

He was late, because of the longer trip and not wanting to push the poor Chrysler too hard. It had been a hot day, the sun was going down in a last begrudging blaze as he drove into the yard. He didn't jump out of the car like a young mechanic full of enthusiasm. The car door sagged open and he just sat there. "Hiya, Kay-Kay," he said in a low voice.

I stared at the dusty, smelly, bushed looking apparition that was supposed to be my husband. "Dear," I cried, "you're covered with sweat and dirt. You

28

look like you've been digging ditches all day!"

He smiled grimly. "That's what I've been doing. Digging ditches."

"You said this job would be electrical work."

"The signals are electrical all right, and they have scads of wires, most of which run underground. The other guys do the connecting. The newer men, like me, dig the trenches. Heck, I could hook up those wires, but there's kind of a seniority system. Everybody has to start on the end of a shovel." He turned wearily in the seat, dropped his feet on the running board. "I just don't understand why those ditches have to be so deep!"

He dug ditches for a week and tossed at night from the ache of tortured muscles. Then they gave him a new task to try out some different muscles. "Today they gave me a machine to drill holes in the rails," he announced, the car door swinging open slowly. "It has a crank you turn with your back. Man, is it hot out on those tracks."

"It's better than digging, isn't it?" I hoped.

"I don't know. You lean over like this . . . oh! The holes are for 'bond' wires at each rail joint, to carry the track current. The signalmen put in the wires. The helper, that's me, drills the holes."

"You did that all day, you poor thing?"

Then he came home smelling of creosote, on top of the sweat and dirt. "Talk about pick and shovel work! We put some special ties in the track today, to mount switch pots on."

"Switch pots?"

"An iron box thing with wires inside. It checks the way the switch is turned, so all have to be right before the signals will clear for trains."

"They loaned me to the signal maintainer. We went six miles out of town on one of those speeders. My job was to walk along the track inspecting those bond wires at each joint. Guess how far I walked."

"Not all the way back?"

"All the way. Six miles."

"Today we dug holes for telephone poles. Don't ever get the idea those poles are standing on top of the ground. Brother!"

"Well, we are back to digging ditches. If it just wasn't so hot."

It was hotter as June began. He came home dusty and fagged out, about the color of a New Mexico Indian, but he got over his discouragement. "The foreman said I was doing all right. I helped hook up the wires and stuff today.

29

This railroad business is interesting. When those trains roll by and you give the engineer a highball, you feel like you're accomplishing something."

"Give him a highball?"

"Slang for get-out-and-go signal, everything O.K."

"Oh."

"Man, I had no idea there was so much to block signals. They break their necks to make sure everything is safe and infallible."

He was cheerful and rapidly becoming as hard as nails, a decided change from the dapper salesman I'd married. He got a pay raise of five cents an hour. Now when they dug ditches he helped lay out the wires. And when they worked on pole lines he climbed the poles, and came home talking confusingly of 'common' and 'AC' and 'drops'.

I didn't know, then, that our future was sealed, or of the unbelievable experiences that lay ahead.

4. The Roses Fade

I knew when I married him that Bill Fisher liked coffee. I didn't realize he wanted three cups at a sitting, at least three times a day. Preferably boiled. In tin cups, I suppose, if I'd stood for it.

"Puts hair on your chest," he assured me.

I didn't consider that likely or desirable. The perking mechanism of our battered aluminum pot had been missing from the start and I'd never really enjoyed my morning coffee.

We were walking along the street past an expensive hardware store on our way to a Sunday afternoon movie. "Bill, look at the coffee pot. Isn't it cute and different? See, it's a drip kind. You remove that metal part after the coffee is made." It was white ceramic intended to resemble a little cobblestone house. On one side was a brown windmill and on the other a pert Dutch girl with a white apron. The top formed the chimney for the house.

"Wouldn't it look darling on our kitchen stove?" I hinted.

"Hmm. Well, I was thinking about paying down on a refrigerator."

That was late in May. My birthday came the first week in June. Bill must have worked hard to get that beautifully wrapped box with a big green bow onto our kitchen table without me seeing it.

"The cobblestone pot!" I cried when I opened the box. "You wonderful husband, you!"

31

"Spent fifteen cents extra to have it gift wrapped."

"It's beautiful. I bet it will make the best coffee you ever tasted. Dear, I'll think of you every time I use it." This to the accompaniment of hugs and kisses.

"If it's that good," he grinned, "the thing is a pretty good investment."

My gift looked so attractive perched on the white electric stove, I did not realize how lucky I was simply to switch a button and start a pot of coffee. Our married life was cruising serenely along; I gave no thought to where it might be cruising. The roses and flowers were blooming in such profusion we were virtually buried in romantic fragrances. Our finances were slowly approaching the credit side. The rent and the electric bill bothered us most, together amounting to twenty-five dollars a month. If we could escape them, I thought, we could have almost everything we needed. But we were happy. Even my aunt began to admit that I might have done worse.

In July we bought a refrigerator. On time, of course, but the salesman said "in a few short months" it would be ours. It was new and glistening, looked beautiful in our little kitchen, and surely helped me to provide more variety in our meals.

But in August the Chrysler began to give us trouble. Bill kept fussing with it. Then one Sunday it stopped dead in the middle of an intersection. Traffic threaded around us while Bill lifted the hood. "Step on the starter," he called. I stepped, but he waved no use. Nervously, he got in and using the starter for power, ground the car off to the side in front of a used car lot. He lifted the hood again and in a minute announced the results. "Distributor shaft gear is stripped; we can't turn a wheel."

"How long will it take to fix?"

"Only a few minutes if I could get a distributor, but on Sunday there isn't much chance." He was perspiring and nervous.

The used car lot owner had been watching, now he walked over to us. He wore a candy-striped shirt, bright red tie and a flat straw hat. "Howdy, folks. Can I be of any help? I'm Harry."

"Yeah," Bill admitted. "Distributor gear is stripped. Have you got something you can push me with, just to get out of your way?"

"Distributor! Well now that's too bad. On Sunday, y'know. Good looking roadster, though. What year is it?"

"Twenty-nine," Bill told him.

"Twenty-nine? Last good ones they made." Harry smiled and tipped his hat to me. "This the missus? Now you folks just relax. I'll get my mechanic to push you around back. Meantime you look around a bit. Check that '38 Buick sedan over there."

Bill didn't want to even look, but we walked around among the cars. The Buick was a black beauty, with five good tires, two windshield wipers, one cracked window and a $400 price tag. Harry reappeared in two minutes but we didn't see any mechanic. "How dya like that one folks?" He jumped in and started the motor. "Where do you work, young fella?"

"Railroad," Bill replied.

Harry's face brightened. "Now I hate to see you folks havin' this trouble. Tell ya what I'll do — you drive this one around the block. If you like it I'll make you a good deal."

Bill hesitated. "What kind of a deal?"

"Twenty-five bucks down and your Chrysler. Thirty-five a month. I'll give you fifty for your car."

We drove the Buick out into the traffic. Bill gunned the motor, tried the brakes several times, then turned into a side street. He got out and lifted the hood, pulled the oil stick and put a drop of oil on his finger. He peered underneath the car, then got back in the driver's seat. "Think we can swing thirty dollars a month, Kay-Kay?"

It would be a fourth of Bill's wages every month. We had the refrigerator payment, rent and electricity, not to mention food.

"Y'know," Bill said, "he knows it won't take much to get the Chrysler running. He can get a hundred and fifty for it."

We drove back to the lot. Bill swung in and parked in the same spot, as if he wouldn't be taking the car. Harry came hurrying out with a paper in his hand. "Got your car in my shop," he beamed. "Now missus, ain't that a nice Buick? Upholstery is perfect. You folks can drive it home today if you say so."

"We can't afford thirty-five a month," Bill told him.

"All right, tell ya what I'll do." Harry didn't even hesitate. "I like you young folks and son, with you workin' for the railroad . . . make it three-fifty and twenty-five a month. Drive it home right now. Missus, you come in tomorrow to fix up the papers and I'll have that cracked window fixed." He wrote on the paper as he talked. "Now son, you give me your boss's name, what department of the railroad and just sign right there."

We didn't buy any groceries but we rode home in style! It had taken every cent in my purse and Bill's 'emergency' ten dollars he carried in his wallet, but the car rode like a dream. Bill put it through its paces, listening for noises. "Pretty extravagant for us, Kay-Kay," he teased, "but it's sure a nice car."

Mrs. L. was flabbergasted when we drove into the yard and Dad came out in his slippers to look it over. I told them how the Chrysler had stopped in traffic and how the man let us drive this home, just because we worked for the railroad. Dad nodded knowingly but made no comment.

RAILROAD. It was a magic word all right. It was written, not only across our credit rating, but right over the honeymoon cottage. In fact it was scrawled right across our marriage.

Another hot day was coming to an end as Bill drove into the yard. He was making better time now, with the Buick. But when I went out to greet him the door swung open ominously. He just sat there with his lunch bucket on his lap.

"Bill, what's happened? What's wrong now?"

"I gotta talk to you, Kay-Kay."

"You haven't been laid off?"

"Worse. I've been promoted to signalman."

"Why, that's wonderful! Why the long face?"

"There is a catch to it." He climbed out of the car and headed for the sanctum for profound discussions, the sofa. I followed anxiously. "Last week the foreman asked me if I thought I could handle a signalman's job. It pays sixty cents an hour. I told him sure I could."

"You've been in the department only four months. You said it might be a year before you got a signalman's rating."

"The job came open for bid and nobody wanted it; and there is a good reason why not. It is eighty miles from here."

It hadn't occurred to me that railroads are hundreds of miles long, and to keep working, he might have to go somewhere else. "Well . . . I guess we could move," I offered.

"Wait until I explain. Sit close to me so I can hold your hand."

I'd never seen him so worried, not even when the Chrysler broke down.

"It is a traveling job," he said. "Moves all over the division . . . and this division is two hundred miles long. That's why nobody wanted it. The work is mostly bonding rails, working with a big track laying gang. I could handle that, and the boss pointed out that I would establish a 'seniority date' that would be very important to me later on. But it means I would be away six days a week . . . only get home on Sundays."

The little house seemed to shudder on its foundation. "Where will you stay during the week?" I wanted to know.

"In an outfit car. That's a railroad camp car, a boxcar with windows, fixed up for single men. I'd have a helper and we'd be batching together."

"You will live in a boxcar?"

He sat holding my hand for a long time. "I don't have to take it, Kay-Kay . . . but I should. The sooner I get a seniority date, the sooner I'll be able to bid for a better position."

Yes, he should take it . . . jobs might be scarce again . . . six months ago

. . . better not think about six months ago . . . "We could try it," I suggested.

"For a few months," he agreed. "By then maybe another chance will come along, closer to home. I'll be getting home on Saturday evenings and be able to stay until Sunday evening."

We sat there thinking about being apart a week at a time. What kind of marriage was that? I tried to remember if there was anything in the marriage vows about how many nights a week he must be home.

"I don't know, dear," my voice was a little shaky, "I just don't know if it would work."

"Sure, it will work, Kay-Kay."

But it didn't work.

He was like a stranger sitting there at the table that first Saturday night. He looked thinner, and browner. He'd said he was glad to be home, and that I looked swell, and I said he was earlier than I'd expected, and he said he sure missed my cooking, and I said the weather had been fine down here. Those were all things we'd saved to say to each other and now they'd been said.

"And what did you do all week?" he asked, trying to be cheerful.

"Monday I cleaned house, even the closet."

"Looks spic and span."

"I helped Tillie in the yard and . . . really, I don't know . . . I just waited for tonight to come."

He told me about the living car, 'outfit', he called it. "It's not bad. More room than here; it has a big kitchen, and windows. It's a baggage car, not a boxcar. I don't like the batching though. Sure missed you, Kay-Kay."

"What kind of bed do you have?"

"Just a steel cot the company furnishes."

"I missed you most at night," I told him. I didn't say I put a pillow on his side to snuggle to, and couldn't get used to the alarm not going off in the mornings.

The night was satisfactory. We tried to prove we were really happy to be together. But we both fell asleep wondering if every week-end would be like this. Through Sunday we tried too hard to please each other. He wanted to relax but he kept watching the time. Sunday night he started back, with a fresh supply of home cooked food, clean laundry, firm little good wishes and what I hoped was enough love to tide him over.

I spent the week listening to everything on the radio, helping Tillie in the garden, trying to convince myself I'd get used to being a grass widow, and wondering if Bill was all right. When Saturday came I was pretty sure the arrangement was going to work.

When Bill came home for another strained week-end he felt the arrangement was not going to work. "It just isn't natural," he argued before he left Sunday evening. "We are just kidding ourselves. Maybe if we'd been married for years it might work . . ."

"The week-ends are so short!" I said. "I keep thinking how soon you'll be going away again, in just a few hours. Then I'll have six whole days to wait for you."

"Kay-Kay, I have an idea." He started the motor of the Buick, and leaned out for a last kiss. "Not enough time to discuss it now. Next trip." Which wasn't the truth, as I found when a thick letter came the following Wednesday.

When Mrs. L. handed me the letter the mailman had put in her rural route box she wondered if something was wrong with our marriage. I, too, wondered why my husband would be writing a letter when he expected to see me in a couple of days. In the privacy of our little cottage I ripped it open anxiously:

"*Dear Kay-Kay: I'm writing this Monday night in hopes you'll have plenty of time to think about what I'm going to say. It's about the idea I mentioned when I was leaving Sunday night.*

"*You and I both know that this system of seeing each other just on week-ends is not going to work. And there is no way we could move every few weeks so we could be near each other.*

"*So I thought why not have you live right up here with me in the outfit car . . .*" I read that line again. It sounded very logical.

"*. . . As I told you, it's not really so bad. The best part is that there is no cost at all. Fuel and electricity are furnished free by the company. There are two cars. One is a boxcar where we keep our tools, track motorcar, the coal and such stuff. The company supplies all the coal we need and the outfit is plenty warm.*

"*If you came up here we'd always be together no matter where they decided to move us. We wouldn't have to pay rent . . .*"

I read that line over twice. The rest of the letter didn't seem to make much difference:

"*. . . Of course, we'll have to accept Thatcher Kelly, my helper living with us. But he's a good guy and he'd help with the food expenses. The scenery and clear air up here are great . . .*"

5. All This And A Star Boarder

The clatter of stove lids and coal bucket awakened me but I wasn't sure where I was. It looked like a steerage cabin on a ship — right next to the engine room — but gray light filtering through lace curtains reminded me; I was in an old railroad car somewhere in the mountains.

"Hey Thatch, get up." Bill's voice came from beyond the partition. It was answered by squeaks from the steel cot.

I realized with a start that the helper's bed was hardly eight feet from ours with only that thin divider between us. I buried my face in Bill's pillow, remembering the frightening night, the trains, the odors.

"Hey Thatch!"

There was a groan and one big squeak, then the sound of a match and the odor of cigarette smoke. Shuffling footsteps went toward the kitchen and down the outside steps. I pounced up, searched for fundamentals of clothing, gasping at the chilliness of the room. In bra and panties, I heard footsteps approaching our boudoir, the thin door opened.

"Eek!" I cried.

"Only me," Bill announced. "Oh, you're up. Sleep all right?"

"Sleep? With all those crazy trains?"

He hesitated uncertainly.

"Don't mind me," I said. "Just my teeth chattering."

"No hurry," my husband said, and left.

For the first time in my life I combed my hair before washing my face. After all, meeting a strange man who had slept at the very bedroom threshold without having washed my face was bad enough. When I went into the next room I was greeted by the aromas of coffee, bacon and cigarette smoke.

"Well, good morning," Bill greeted. "Kay, this is Thatch."

He was a tall rangy boy about nineteen with neatly combed sandy hair and blue eyes. He wore leather boots, blue work shirt and jeans.

"Howdy, ma'am." His manner showed he'd been taught respect for 'women folk' but he was very self-conscious. "Hope I didn't disturb ya when I came in last night."

"All I can say is you should oil the springs of that cot sometime. Doesn't it keep you awake?"

He looked at me in surprise. "Nothing keeps me awake, ma'am."

I wondered if I could depend on that. "Those trains would drive anybody nuts," I declared. "How do you two sleep up here?"

"You'll get used to them," Bill put in.

"But those fast ones are terrible!"

"They're the passengers. Don't worry about it. Come on and have some breakfast."

My husband's prowess at cooking was quite amazing. Thatch started on a plateful of bacon and eggs like he hadn't eaten for a week. That, or the mountain air was stirring my own appetite. I sat down at the oil-cloth-covered table and poured a cup of coffee. Taken in one of their heavy mugs, it had a certain campfire bite to it.

"Have some eggs," Bill said. "Little nourishment will help you forget about last night."

"I might try one. You've fried enough for an army."

But I hadn't figured on Thatch. He was sliding his third and fourth onto the plate. I reminded myself to ask Bill how much he would pay for board. Finally satisfied, our star boarder stood up, stretched in apparent dislike of having to go to work, and lighted a cigarette. "Shore glad you came up, ma'am."

"Well, thank you. You can call me Kay."

"Okay, I will."

"Why are you glad I came up, Thatch?"

"Oh, I dunno. Better than doin' our own cooking. Won't be any dishes in the sink tonight, I betcha."

So that was the real reason they wanted me up here!

After Thatch had put on a heavy jacket with too short sleeves Bill handed

The large track-laying gang coming in from work.   (*Robert DelCarlo collection*)

him their lunch buckets. "Go bring the motorcar down the main to here. I'll be ready then." When he was gone Bill put on his coat, found his gloves, then took me in his arms. "We'll be back by four-thirty, Kay-Kay. Hope you won't get lonesome. Not much to do around here."

"At least I'll have a radio. If I can get Sally's Other Husband I'll feel more at home. She hasn't anything compared to this."

He looked bewildered. Outside we heard a sound like a truck motor. "There goes the steel gang." He jerked open the door before I could protest and about forty men stared in. They were seated on a slow-moving string of track cars, collars turned up and caps down, but all interested in the view.

"You might as well have kissed me in the open doorway! I'm accustomed to privacy, Bill Fisher. I'm a woman, remember."

"Ah Kay-Kay, people are different up here. They don't think about such things." He kissed me hopefully and pulled on his gloves. Outside, Thatch was sitting on a tiny orange-color speeder, looking cold in the frosty air and embarrassed at the tender love scene. Bill said, "Bye."

"Bye." I tried to sound happy.

The door stuck; the small window rattled when I slammed it. In the living room I sat down in one of the weathered chairs, looked at the drab walls, the steel cot, pot-bellied stove with its coal bucket. So this was an 'outfit car', something that moved, that came with my husband's job.

At the foot of Thatch's cot was a small table with a dozen magazines, metal ashtray, the table radio. A cord ran from the overhead light socket down behind the curtain rod to the radio. The curtains were a dark green burlap. Two battered kerosene lamps were nailed at head height, one on each side of the room.

39

The pot-bellied stove tried to welcome me but on the wall above Bill's desk a girl-calendar gave me the cold shoulder. She was a baby-faced redhead with silly pink panties and a revealing bra. She was holding a telephone in a pose that looked awfully tiresome. I found a pencil on the desk, got up and marked off yesterday and today. Bill said we'd try it for three weeks. I had nineteen days left!

Nineteen days — and nights — among the trains, mountains and Mexicans; and no telling what else. I could never tell Aunty what it was like. She wouldn't believe me! The naked girl smiled at me. I drew a moustache on her and sat down again.

The only thing which seemed to be a logical reason for it all was Bill's desk. It was really another small table and a series of shelves nailed to the wall, divided into pigeon holes. I took a paper from one of the niches. It was a carbon copy in Bill's scrawl:

"Daily Work Report — New Rail Bonding, Curve 393 West. 160 bond wires, 320 ch pins, two insulated joints, 131RE." I tried another niche.

"Monthly Outfit Report — Living Car No. 713. Condition: Good. Tool & Material Car No. 787. Condition: Roof leaks." Judging from back reports, the roof of the 787 had leaked for seven months. Reports prior to August were signed by R. Ramgaw. I wondered why neither of them had been able to fix the leaky roof. In another niche I found a small book; Rules & Regulations. This, then, was the famous 'Book of Rules'.

"Safety is of first importance in the discharge of duty.

"Employees must pass the required examinations.

"Employees must show their watches and watch certificates to division officers and watch inspectors upon request."

There were sections headed; Track, Roadbed, Ballast, Gauge, Crossings, Signals, Organization and Supervision . . . Bill had said there were over two hundred rules covering everything but an engineer sneezing! How did they ever find time to run trains? It even showed twenty different things an engineer could say with his whistle. Suddenly I dropped the book.

Someone was on top of the roof. It sounded like they were dragging a long rope. I sat petrified as footsteps shuffled back and forth, then faded away. Next I heard the sound of gurgling water in the ceiling tanks in our kitchen; it hadn't occurred to me they had to be filled occasionally.

I ran down the steps and out onto the tracks far enough to see on top of the baggage car. Nobody up there, but a hose was stuck into a pipe projecting from the curved roof. It trailed from one car to the next as far as I could see it. A drizzling rain and cold fog had started so I gave up looking for our mysterious serviceman. In the kitchen, the gurgling continued until water gushed down the outside of the car. This evidently was a signal for the hose man to shut off the flow. Now I'll see who he is — but the footsteps didn't return.

You don't wash dishes with cold water. And if someone has just filled the tanks you have nothing but cold water. That apparently was Lesson One in Life In Outfit Car.

The only solution seemed to be, stir up the fire and wait. The fire in the cookstove had burned down to few glowing coals and when I threw in a scoop of coal a stinking gray smoke billowed up. It took more skill than I suspected for several lumps clattered across the floor, leaving a trail of sandy grime. So now where was the broom? It was kept, I discovered, in our attached boxcar, the 787 with a leaky roof.

Except for the fact you reached it by skittering across a loose plank laid over the couplings, the arrangement was much like having a closed back porch. There was even a set of double washtrays but no faucets. The broom, mop and mop bucket stood in one corner against a huge bin full of coal, and there was a battered old icebox for our meat and vegetables. Hung on spikes were some rainclothes, a pair of hip boots, and two dusty lawn chairs. I peered beyond a passage around the coal bin.

Lighted by two small dingy windows high in each wall, the rest was like a big cluttered barn. Only the center, between the heavy sliding doors, was clear. The far end was crammed with lumber, cubicles of tools, many large spools of wire, coils of rope hanging from hooks, and even overhead racks of some sort of long scoops and poles. I decided that 'tool car' was an understatement.

With my fire burning merrily, the floor reasonably clean again, and the radio tuned to Sally's Other Husband, I settled down to my fate.

"Sally, we must get married . . . now," John said.

"But what about your mother's illness, John?"

"We'll just have to break the news to her gently."

"No, John, think of the shock." Sally was crying softly. What would her decision be? I heard a train coming; the glass in the door began to rattle.

"John, I . . . " I ran to the radio and put my ear against it but all I heard were the crashing exhausts of the passing engine. As that gave way to squealing boxcars the announcer's voice came in weakly. "Listen tomorrow to Sally's Other Husband, brought to you by Wonder Soap; the soap that soothes the dirt out of . . ."

"Darn the trains!" My vocabulary in describing trains was destined to become more explicit, but at the moment this was only my first experience at frustration. But Bill's comment that there wasn't much to do up here didn't quite hold up. Hardly had the boxcars and their two helper engines gone on to wherever they were going, when I heard a knock at our door. There was a man . . . a Mexican there . . . wearing the biggest, blackest hat I'd ever seen. I backed away.

"Buenas dias, Senora!" He walked right in carrying a box of kindling wood.

"Who . . . what do you want?"

"I bring you wood," he grinned. "You need 'em maybe." His teeth were just as straight and even as the rows of sticks in the box which he placed on the kitchen floor. I looked at the box, filled to the brim with perfectly straight sticks. He started back down the steps.

"Thanks very much," I called.

He stopped at the foot of the steps, relieved that I hadn't slammed the door. "Gracias, Senora," he smiled. "Anything you want, I catch 'em."

"Did you put water in our tanks a while ago?"

"Si, Senora."

"That was you on top of the roof!"

"Oh si, me," he grinned.

Feeling much like a girl in a western movie, I was a little sorry I hadn't been more cordial. There was too much to learn in this 'outfit car'.

When Bill came in the first thing he saw was the box of kindling . . . before he even saw me. "Where did that come from?" he asked.

"Now I like that. Aren't you even going to kiss me first?"

"Oh sure." He glanced at Thatch getting out of his wet coat and then kissed me haphazardly.

"Well, aren't you glad I'm still here?" I demanded. "I could have walked down and taken a bus home, you know."

"'Course I'm glad."

Thatch went out to the tool car so Bill kissed me again, better. "I'm just not used to doing that with him watching."

"But you don't mind going to bed with me, and him listening six feet away."

"All right, let's skip it for now," he spluttered as Thatch reappeared. But apparently they were both glad to see me, to find the outfit warm and supper started. They were amazed that the Mexican had filled the tanks and brought kindling. His name, Bill explained, was Candy, for Candelario. He was a nice old guy but not exactly an angel. He ran a poker game in his spare time . . . and not just for fun.

Bill climbed into bed happily that night and put his arms around me. "Well, you've been in the outfit twenty-four hours. What do you think?"

Beyond the partition Thatch had the radio going, discreetly waiting for our light to go out. I supposed he was still trimming his nails with a pocketknife, his main occupation all evening. I thought about last night, the trains, the squeaks, the red can. Like an Apache brave long away from his squaw, my husband had romantic ideas but he found me anything but receptive.

"I don't know, Bill. This going to bed is the worst part."

"You'll get used to it." Then he whispered cutely, "We can wait for a train to come along." That was a new idea! I had to admit this husband of mine was resourceful if not a little primitive. With the mention of trains, I wondered what the night would be like.

It turned out to be gruesome. I was frightened, my husband disappointed, and Thatch no doubt embarrassed. But the trains came and went on their terrifying relentless way. With daylight I awoke from a fitful sleep, to the same tune of banging stove lids and coal buckets. I was nervous, exhausted and ready to tell Bill to have the minister give back his two bucks.

If I'd learned anything the first twenty-four hours, it was only a small beginning. I got the impression I was expected to be up as soon as Bill had fires going, on my toes, ready to help with breakfast and make lunches. If Thatch were still in bed and had to dress practically in front of me, I was to ignore that. But I found that mornings up in the mountains were clear and beautiful. Peeking out I saw the trees standing rigidly in frosty coats and the canyon below white with pre-dawn vapors. I even began to take interest in the big gang getting their motorcars and tools ready to go.

Bill seemed more concerned about my feelings and how I'd slept, so I decided to wait a day or two to mention returning the two bucks, but I marked the day on the calendar with a good firm stroke.

My education, like the trains, went right on. I learned that Mr. Candy planned to fill our tanks every morning just before I was ready to wash dishes. He expected me to use all the kindling he could carry, and was disappointed if the box wasn't empty.

"Use pulenty," he advised. "Make fire hot quick."

He left another box and went away. In a minute he was back with a chunk of ice. I had to show him where the icebox was so I knew Bill hadn't received all this service. "Pretty soon no more ice," he informed me.

I thought he meant winter would come; I learned later the railroad supplied ice until a certain date in September and then stopped, whether the temperature was hot or cold.

One day Mr. Candy didn't show up. After Sally's Other Husband I walked along the string of fifteen outfits. I found him sawing wood at a huge pile of ties.

"Hello," I said. "Buena dia."

"Como esta, Senora! You speak Spanish now."

"That's all I know. You didn't come this morning."

43

"Too busy yet. No more coal, gotta cut wood. Boss says coal comin' but I think he donno when."

I asked him how he filled our water tanks. He pointed to a huge tank car with a pump mounted on one end. Long hoses ran from the pump over the tops of the cars. "Lotsa pump-em," he said.

"You have to fill all these cars?"

"Oh si, Senora. Ever day. Mexican boys use lotta water."

I made a mental note to conserve water.

"Cooky, too," Mr. Candy added.

"They cook in the cars?"

"No, Senora. China boy cook."

So I met Cooky, a Chinese about thirty with buck teeth and straight black hair. He spoke very loud garbled English and apparently very loud garbled Spanish. I think he and Mr. Candy swore at each other continuously, but I couldn't understand them.

"You cook 'em outfit?" Cooky asked. "What gang?"

"No, I'm wife. Signalman outfit." This pidgin English was catching.

"You wife? No good. All time cook, no pay."

Maybe he had something there! Nevertheless Cooky, Mr. Candy and I became good friends, and I went back to the 713 carrying a luscious berry pie and a loaf of homemade bread. Both of them seemed to have a lot of respect for me because I chose to live with my husband in an outfit car.

I learned too, that week, that freight trains have conductors as well as passenger trains, and that the caboose was the conductor's castle. That 'car' meant outfit, boxcar or motorcar but not an automobile, and a 'light engine' was a helper engine returning loose without any train. 'Light' also was something you forgot when you went out to the dreamhouse in the dark.

There was one train different than all the rest, the local freight. It had a smaller engine, seldom more than ten cars, and ran 'down' on Monday, Wednesday, Friday, and 'up' on the other days with no apparent schedule. It stopped to unload supplies for Mr. Candy to lug in. He referred to the train as "deloco". The expression not only described the stubby train — it seemed to fit almost everything connected with this pioneer existence.

6. Another Woman!

Monday, the 11th day. Sally's Other Husband was on. Sally was saying, "No, John, I'll never be able to marry you." Thatch hadn't made his bed; he'd come in about daylight, laid down under the top blanket with his clothes on. Bill had to shake him awake.

"But Sally, I can't go on without you."

"Oh John, darling, it's not just us. Think of your mother . . ."

Someone was rapping loudly on my door. It didn't sound like Mr. Candy. When I opened the door there was a woman. She was smiling as she said, "Hello. Can I come in?" She was wearing a print house dress under her coat; was about thirty-five, short, stocky, on the blonde side. She had a bag of knitting.

"Yes, of course . . . come in," I stammered in surprise.

She dropped her knitting on a kitchen chair and took off her coat. "I'm Madge Nichols. My husband is Roscoe; he knows your husband. We're a welding gang." The radio was blaring the wonders of WONDER SOAP so I went in and shut it off. "I missed Sally's Other Husband," she went on. "Did she accept him finally?"

"Not yet," I told her.

"It'll go on for days like that. I get so mad but I don't dare miss it." She had a quick happy laugh and nice teeth. Her eyes were brown, in a round face. "Our outfits are moving in here today from Norden," she continued. "Your

45

husband told mine about you being here, so I thought I'd stop and get acquainted. Norden is a lousy place. Ever been there?"

"No, this is my first experience in an outfit car."

"It is!" She looked around, peeked into the other room. "Gawd, I wish I was just starting. No, I don't either. You got a swell car if you want to fix it up. Baggage cars are way the best. Coaches are the worst; all those windows. No place to hang anything unless you board up part of them and then they look like hell. How long you been here?"

"Just a week."

"A week? Gawdamighty, no wonder you haven't fixed it up. I'd paint this kitchen and . . . say what's your name?"

"Just call me Kay. Would you like some coffee? It tastes so good up here; it must be the air."

"The water, kid. That's one good thing about the mountains. You bet I'll have coffee." She looked in the other room. "Who sleeps there, Kay?"

"My husband's helper," I said reluctantly.

"And your room is on the end?" She noticed the thin partition and was thinking . . . I wondered what she was thinking. She chattered on, unconcerned. "As I was saying, Norden is a lousy place. You're stuck in the snowsheds and can't see a darned thing, can't walk anywhere without going through the sheds. It's the coldest place this side of hades . . . what a cute coffee pot!"

"Do you like it? Bill gave it to me on my birthday."

"I wish Roscoe would do something like that. He either gives me jewelry or a radio. I never get to wear the jewelry and he listens to the radio as much as me. He gives me radios 'cause ours is always getting wrecked."

"Wrecked?" I had visions of them throwing radios at each other.

"From being in the outfit," she explained. "Either they bang the car and knock it off, or the vibration — we got cast iron wheels, you got good steel wheels on your car — or they spur you out where there is bum electricity, or you get lightning." She talked about her husband's work, welding up rail ends which became battered from the constant pounding of train wheels on the track joints. He had three helpers to handle all the equipment and I meant to ask where they slept, but didn't get the chance. I had to stop her, though, when she said, "We just moved off McKinney. He's a stinker."

"What do you mean by moved off him?"

"Moved off his district. He's the roadmaster from Troy east."

"Oh." The term roadmaster was familiar; I'd seen it in that rule book.

"The roadmaster is boss of all the track forces working on his district," she explained, "but not you. Your husband answers to the signal supervisor."

I supposed that was important to know. But I was lost again when she started on about 'system' seniority. Evidently that meant they might work anywhere on the company's system of lines, while Bill had a 'division' job.

"Helluva lot better," she declared. "You'll never move more than two hundred miles, that's for sure."

"Two hundred miles?" I cried.

"That's nothing. Roscoe and I moved six hundred miles in one jump. That's when it's bad. Sometimes you get stuck for days in a big terminal, or if they decide your outfit needs fixing, it might be two weeks."

I wondered how long it would take to learn all these odd things. "Madge," I said cautiously, "how long have you lived in an outfit?"

"Ten years."

"Ten years!"

Madge Nichols; peppy, blonde, capable. Yes, capable of walking into my baggage car a perfect stranger, to welcome me to life along the railroad — and then blandly flooring me by saying she'd lived in an outfit for ten years. Were all these railroaders misfits, nomads? Was my husband one, too? "Haven't you ever thought about living in a house?" I asked her.

"Oh, sure. Roscoe wants to, but not me. I like traveling. He's knocked around a lot but I always lived in one town, Tucson. He met me there when I was a waitress."

"But don't you get tired of this existence?"

"Oh, sometimes. But I married the guy, so I asked for it. Hey, here's the work train already!" She jumped up and opened the door.

An engine was stopping on the downhill track with a dozen oddly mixed cars; some with steam shovels on them and some that looked like dump cars, a dilapidated caboose and some boxcar outfits, one red tank car. The train had arrived so quietly I hadn't heard it. How she had, or knew it was the work train was beyond me. The engine suddenly whistled toot-to-to-to.

"They got to crossover to get into this spur," Madge said.

Whether she knew that from the whistle, or some other way, was also a mystery. "Is that your outfit, Madge?" I asked.

"Them four is ours, including the tank car. Mine is the one on this end. That last one is for the helpers."

That explained where her husband's helpers slept. Could Bill get another car too? The train now began backing up through the switches onto the uphill track. I said, "I thought you had a passenger coach."

"Ah, they condemned our coach four years ago. Sent it to the burn-up yard without even telling us. Gave us that darned boxcar instead."

The train had backed past us and stopped. Now it was moving downhill again but had left her four cars standing alone on the main track. A brakeman threw a switch, and apparently another released some brakes, for her cars began to coast by themselves. Like toy cars, they trundled over the switch into the track our outfits were on, and came to a stop.

"Just as I figured! Come on, Kay." She ran down the steps and toward the train crew. "Hey, hold it there." The train stopped. When I reached her side between her outfits and a big steam shovel, she was belligerently facing a brakeman in striped overalls and cap. He held a thick short club, as in self-defense. "Did you see that culvert on the other side?" she shot at him. She leaned down and pointed under her car. "What's the idea of spotting us with the side door right over that hole?"

"Sure I saw it," he replied. "You got a door on this side, ain'tcha?"

"The one on that side is the backdoor." She drew herself up until she almost reached to his chin. "Do you want me to tell you why we go out the backdoor sometimes?"

He opened his mouth, hesitated, then stepped onto the caboose and waved a signal with his stick. The whole train began backing up again. Up beyond the spur switch it stopped and the engine eased into the spur, touched Madge's four cars and pushed them another six feet.

The brakeman waited. Madge surveyed under the car critically, then nodded OK. The crew strode toward their train without looking at us, but when the engine trundled past, the engineer was grinning. Madge glowered at him like a dowdy little hen who had just run off a wolfhound.

"You got to get tough with them," she fumed. "They don't give a damn who has to live in these outfits. Well, would you like to see my car?"

"You haven't any steps," I replied. "I can get the camp man to set them up."

"Never mind. You might as well learn how to do it alone, Kay." She grabbed a rung of the iron ladder bolted to the wall and gave a leap, landing expertly on the first rung fully three feet off the ground. She opened her door and looked down at me. "Try it. Come on."

I grasped the iron ladder and tried to swing my feet up. They missed by a wide margin.

"You're stiff as a board," she laughed. "Throw yourself like you are going to vault clean over the car."

Wishing for a pair of slacks, I heaved again, missed, and nearly broke both arms. "I'll practice later," I told her.

"You'll learn, or wait all day sometime," she commented. "Here come the steps, city gal." She thumped around inside and out shot a set of the cumbersome portable steps like ours, the feet ramming into the ground in exactly the right position. I mounted them gingerly but they were solid. In the middle of her floor was another set.

Madge said, "Here, you put this set out the back door. You might as well learn." She opened the door. "Now drag them around so one end is sticking out the doorway, keep them straight."

With her help I shoved and pushed the heavy things until she was satisfied.

"Now pick up the back end and shove, straight as you can. All right, lift."

"Oooh!" I groaned, as every female tendon in me protested. The end of the steps rose slowly off the floor, then suddenly overbalanced and shot out of my grasp. There was a clunk against the side of the car. Madge looked out as my head spun dizzily.

"Perfect," she announced.

So this was life in an outfit. If I'd been a lady wrestler I might make it. But when I got my breath and looked around, I was amazed at her kitchen. Starched muslin curtains in red-green fiesta print outlined the windows. The cookstove, a farmhouse type on cast legs, gleamed of polished nickel and silky black surfaces. Her cupboards were painted light green with cheery dime-store decalcomanias. A round table and four chairs painted white stood opposite a real refrigerator.

"Madge, how cute and cheerful. Did you and your husband do all this?"

"I did most of it," she declared. "Come see the living room."

It was really a living room. Linoleum on the floor but softened with throw rugs, a wicker settee with full cushions, an overstuffed chair, a floor lamp. In one corner the inevitable pot-bellied stove but across the far end was a handsome bookcase. It all was cozy, but rather crowded.

"The only bad thing is the windows," Madge said.

Yes, the windows. She'd made short imitation drapes but the effect was still discouraging. Four of them, two on each side, were small and set high up in the wall, as if the designer had a monastery in mind. Directly below them were four more, scarcely two feet off the floor, partially blocked by furniture. "Why, people can look in but you can't look out," I said.

"Absolutely silly," she agreed, "but most of the boxcar outfits are made that way. Damned if I know why."

Instinctively my gaze turned upwards, and I knew I was in a boxcar. The divided ceiling tapered down from each side of a center beam, and nailed to the beam was the electrical conduit, with a branch pipe running down each wall to an outlet. Yet the room looked comfortable. I could picture her husband relaxing in the overstuffed chair while she stretched out on the settee. I started to sit down in the big chair.

"Wait, Kay, my radio!" She jerked up the big cushion; under it the radio was hiding cozily. "Haven't had one broken since I tried this idea."

"But Madge, what about your floor lamp standing there?"

"Ha! I'm surprised you thought of it. I fixed that for sure. Look, screwed to the floor." She untangled the radio cord and plugged it in, but there was no sound. "Nuts, I'm getting thick-headed. No juice hooked up yet. Well, we can go over to your place and listen to the radio. Okay?"

"Yes, certainly," I agreed. My place, her place, as if we lived in houses with foundations instead of wheels, with ground under our feet instead of tracks.

She calmly decided she would use our 'privy' until Roscoe got 'home'. If this was home, for ten years? Well, I wondered . . . But she was pleased when I asked to see the rest of her car.

With the kitchen in the middle of the car, the bedroom had to be in the opposite end from the living room. There was a short hallway arrangement formed by a shower room and two closets. The bedroom was attractive but crowded by a double bed, chest of drawers and two chairs. Two windows in the same weird arrangement were covered with organdy curtains. In the middle of the bed lay a large round mirror with pillows piled on it.

"This is how you save your mirror," she explained, moving the pillows and hanging the framed glass on a hook in the end wall.

"Is it really that bad," I asked her.

"You'll find out, kid. 'Course being a division outfit you won't move in through freights. Why, once they tore our water tanks right out of the ceiling. Now we drain 'em every time."

Back in the kitchen, she showed me how all the cupboards had hasps and locks, how she had stuffed towels between the stacks of dishes for this move today. Even the refrigerator had a lock and was bolted to the wall.

How could she be so enthusiastic — after ten years?

Madge stayed at 'my place' all afternoon but I don't think she heard the radio programs; she was better than any soap opera. She told of being in the Southwest for several years where desert sand blew in through the cracks of her outfit, of endless flat country where the trains rocked her car as they roared by at sixty miles an hour, and of humid valleys with lettuce fields and mosquitoes that swarmed in sloughs along the track.

"Kid, you won't find a better division than this," she assured me. "These mountains can't be beat."

When Bill came in from work he knew we were getting new neighbors. He explained that Roscoe's crew would be working with the track gang for a while. Roscoe, he said, was a nice guy and a hard working son-of-a-gun. "What's she like?" he wanted to know.

I described Madge and how she'd walked right in to get acquainted, and about going to her car. I told him how they had it fixed up comfortably, and all I'd learned about their having a system job. It dawned on me that I was actually sounding enthusiastic. Then I added, "Bill, they've been in outfits for ten years!"

"Criminy, I didn't know that. Ten years?"

Pacific Limited westbound near Crystal Lake.   *(Photo courtesy Southern Pacific)*

The Nichols were a godsend, though. It seemed more civilized to have some neighbors besides Mr. Candy and Cooky. Of course she came over every morning after she'd done her 'house cleaning', and I'd go to her car in the afternoon. When the weather was sunny we'd walk a mile or so up the track, or take the

Buick down to Cisco for groceries. I noticed Mr. Candy still brought me kindling but didn't take her any.

They invited us to the outfit one evening to play cards, and it quickly became a habit. The men: Roscoe, Bill, Thatch, and one of their crew named Johnny Beverly played pinochle at the kitchen table drawn into the middle of the room, while she and I sat in the living room. Madge could carry on a conversation with me, listen to the radio, and still follow the game.

It sounded crazy to me, the way partners talked back and forth about their hands and expressions like 'a hundred aces and sixty queens', The only game I knew was bridge. But apparently it was exciting because almost every game someone would slam down a final card and holler, "There by God!"

"Nobody on the railroad plays bridge," Madge told me. "It's pinochle from one end of the road to the other."

Roscoe was about ten years older than she, stocky and muscular, sandy-haired. His teeth were crooked and cigarette stained but his smile was always a happy grin. He laughed in a half coughing way at everything amusing and carried on a continuous kidding with Thatch about being from back on the farm. One evening, when I said I liked their outfit, he replied, "I'm getting awful tired of it, though. About ready to bid off somewhere."

"Ah baloney," Madge countered. "Kay, he's been saying that for five years. He just likes the overtime on this job."

I decided that Roscoe Nichols was slightly hen-pecked.

The helper, Johnny Beverly, had eye trouble. When I met him the first night I was glad I wasn't wearing a sweater, and I think he was sorry. It would have saved him time. He had almost black eyes and black hair, a handsome jaw and profile, and evidently knew it. He was about twenty-eight, tanned and healthy, with large even teeth. He cataloged me instantly, glanced at Bill, and then settled back on Madge. He usually placed his chair so he could see her. I wondered, oddly, if he really felt she was the more attractive.

Madge mentioned one day that Johnny was a big break for Roscoe. He was a good welder, had quit once and lost his seniority, so had to re-hire as an apprentice. "He'll probably bid on the first regular welder's job that comes open," she added. "Then Roscoe'll lose him."

Or did she mean that she would lose him?

7. I Lose My Rose Colored Glasses

The next Saturday was payday. With it came an incident that shocked me in a way that made trains and privies seem trivial. Those things could be picturesque if you imagined you were in a movie, but this was frightening, sickening, and for real.

The roadmaster had come along on a motorcar that afternoon delivering paychecks. He stopped and paid Mr. Candy and Cooky. I wondered if he would give me ours, but Madge said the boys had to sign for them personally. Bill had his when he came home.

Thatch and all of Roscoe's men left right after work, in a hurry to spend their checks. After dinner we went over to Nichols' for visiting and cards. Bill and Roscoe tried to teach me pinochle but I was a poor student. Once during the evening we heard the gang singing loudly in Spanish. Even in such a ribald chorus the songs had a romantic lilt.

Bill said, "It beats me how they can get drunk so soon after getting paid."

We stayed late, talking over a midnight lunch. Bill and I started homeward, picking our way along the ties with the always handy flashlight. He said it felt like rain. Suddenly we heard someone running toward us in the darkness. Whoever it was saw our light and slid to a stop in the gravel. We could hear him breathing heavily a few feet away.

"What the hell .. ?" Bill swung the beam of his light and caught the figure of a man crouching, staring at us.

"Look at him!" I cried. His hair was disheveled, shirt torn to shreds. He stood like a man desperate, ready to fight for his life. One hand, covered with blood, clutched his upper right arm. Blood was dripping from his gory right hand clenched around . . ."Oh, Bill, he's got a knife!"

The man stood at bay, glancing backward over his shoulder, afraid of something behind him, afraid of this light in his face. He held the knife poised in that awful dripping hand. I wanted to scream, run . . . He took a step toward us.

"Cual es?" Bill snapped, holding the light on him.

"Oh, senor Beel!" Recognition dawned on him slowly, then his manner changed to pleading. "Mi brazo . . ." He babbled in rushing Spanish, gesturing with his injured arm so that the knife flashed.

Bill ordered sharply, "Bajar la . . . lo cuchillo."

The fellow stared down at the knife as if he didn't know he still held it. He threw it on the ground.

"It's all right, Kay. He's been hurt pretty bad." Bill walked slowly toward the fellow, stepping on the knife as he did so, and examined the cut arm with his flashlight. "This guy is liable to bleed to death if somebody doesn't help him. I'll take him to his foreman. No, it's Saturday, the foreman is gone." He herded the man toward the foot of our steps, then said curtly, "Entrar, amigo."

"You're not taking him into our outfit?"

"Sure. If I take him to his own bunkcar the fight might start all over again. We can't let him stand here and die! Go in and turn on the lights."

"No siree, I'm not going in there with him behind me!"

"For gosh sake, he won't hurt anybody now."

"He'll drip blood all over," I cried, my stomach turning over at the very thought.

"Put some newspapers on the floor," Bill exclaimed.

"But that knife . . ."

"He's forgotten about it. Go ahead before he gets some wild idea."

I ran up the steps, found the light and some newspapers. I scattered them around the floor but already the fellow had dripped a little red pool where he stood in the doorway. Now he appeared really horrible. Blood-stained remains of his shirt hung on bare powerful shoulders, flapping as he swayed. Liquor fumes soaked the air, mixed with the odor of sweat. His face was scary, the lower lip cut and terribly swollen. His blood went tap, tap, tap on the papers.

Bill slammed the door and jerked a chair out onto the papers. "Sentarse," he said, and the man quickly sat down.

"I don't know why you brought him in here!" I cried hysterically. A fearful gash ran from just under his large muscle down his arm and off at the wrist. He sat there with his hand palm up, a crimson drop hanging on each finger.

"Get some clean towels or pillowcases for bandages," Bill ordered.

His harsh words kept me from fainting. I rushed into the bedroom and grabbed two pillowcases. The midnight lunch was in my throat as I handed them to Bill through the doorway, but he threw them right back at me.

"Rip them up. I'm busy."

He had used his handkerchief for a tourniquet and was holding it tight with one hand while he ripped the soaked sleeve off. Now he used a piece of pillowcase seam to form a fresh one. "This guy's in bad shape, he needs a doctor. Sorry if it bothers you."

"It's all right," I said meekly, tearing bandages in the living room. The man was groaning. I couldn't look at the back of his head without feeling dizzy. The forbidding drip, drip had stopped and Bill was drawing water in a washpan.

"Here are the bandages," I said, dropping them hastily on the kitchen table. Where Bill was mopping the blood away I could see muscle and ligaments exposed. I ran back into the other room.

"Wait a minute, where are you going? Go and tell Roscoe what happened. Have him go up to the switch shanty and phone the constable." Thankful for the chance to get away, I hurried to the door. Bill hollered, "Take the flashlight! It's in my hip pocket."

Madge came to the door in her robe. "Gawdamighty, you're white as a sheet. What in hell's wrong, Kay?"

I gasped out the news. She called, "Roscoe, c'mere!" I promptly vomited all over her steps.

When I could talk again Roscoe had his coat on. I said, "I'm sorry about your steps . . ."

"Don't worry about the steps. Is this guy cut bad, you say?"

"Bill says so. He bled something awful."

"O.K." He stepped out and jumped from the steps.

I said, "Madge, can I stay here with you? Oh, I'll clean your steps . . ."

"Will you quit worrying about the steps. Gawd, I'll fix that in a jiffy." She yanked a bucket from under the sink, drew it full of water and sloshed them down, then went back for another bucketful. "All right. Now you can stay here if you want to, but this I gotta see."

There was nothing to do but follow her. I felt sick and meeker than ever against her bravery but when we happened on the man's knife lying in the gravel, she said, "Gawd, did he have that?"

"In his hand. We met right here in the dark."

"We met right here in the dark!" I told Madge.

"I'd have crapped my pants!" she declared. She kicked the sticky weapon into the weeds. Her frank comment made me feel a lot better.

Bill finished wrapping the man's arm while Madge sat enthralled on a kitchen chair. Shortly Roscoe joined us. With the last of my pillowcases used up, the man stood uncertainly. "Gracias, senor."

"No, estarse." Bill pulled his chair off the papers and pointed to it. The man sat down again, held there by the sheer weight of our numbers, his face still dirty with dried sweat and his hair disheveled.

We were talking, virtually ignoring the poor fellow, when the knock came. Bill opened the door and a voice said, "Where's the guy who was in a fight?" Two men came in.

The constable was raw-boned, tall and mean looking. He wore tan riding clothes, Stetson hat and a gun in a shiny leather holster. The deputy looked much like a cowpuncher in jeans. He was medium height, with a bored expression. The constable glared at the injured man, who was now fear-stricken.

Bill said, "He needs medical attention. Lost a lot of blood."

"Why can't they do these things in the daytime?" the officer growled. "Did he say who did it?"

56

"I didn't ask him," Bill replied.

"Well, ask him."

Bill tried in halting Spanish. The fellow assumed his pleading attitude again, rattling incoherently. Bill said, not unkindly, "Despacio, compadre." The words came more slowly. "He says it was the camp man, Candelario."

"Not Mr. Candy," I objected. "It couldn't be him!"

The constable swung around. "Who are you?"

"Take it easy," Bill shot back. "She's my wife. Will you guys kindly take over so we can go to bed? All we know is we found the guy outside bleeding to death."

"All right, Buster. No need to get rough." He drew his gun and motioned to the injured man. As they went out the door he said, "This sort of stuff is no picnic, y'know. I don't know any Spanish."

"I don't either," Bill said, shutting the door.

After they and the Nichols were gone Bill bundled up the papers, took them out between the tracks and set fire to them. Coming back he looked for the knife with the flashlight.

"Madge kicked it over there," I said from the doorway.

He found it, examined it for a minute, then threw it as hard as he could into the blackness of the canyon. Next he scrubbed out the washpan and only then did my stomach begin to cease quivering. My husband put his arm around me. "Kind of a rough deal for you, Kay, but don't let it worry you. These laborers are that way when they are drunk, but they keep to themselves. They'll avoid women, especially Americanos."

I was a long time getting to sleep, and heard the first train a long way off. It drew closer, thundering up the track. I was anxious for it to go by, so I'd hear if someone were out there. When the night was quiet again I could picture that man glaring at us with wild eyes and a knife. I wondered if Bill had cleaned the spots on the floor. Another train came along. Hours later it began to rain.

Heavy, rustling drops came in fitful bursts. The rain ran down the sides of the outfit and dripped on the ground. Then it hailed. If he'd been out in that with his arm bleeding and no hat or coat...Bill wanted me to stay with him...What about this terrible experience tonight? Maybe I took things too seriously. Maybe I should feel more like Madge; no rose-colored glasses. "I married the guy, so I asked for it." If I stayed would I become like her?

The rain settled to a steady drumming with gusts of wind. Number 88 whistled far off and came tearing by on a dead run. It whistled again as it

57

raced through the rain. I admired Madge for her ruggedness but not the profanity. If I could have one without the other . . .

It would be exciting, staying here with Bill, learning all about railroading, and mountains, and life without rose-colored glasses. Funny, people riding on trains never knew all this was necessary to give them comfort and service. It would be interesting for a while . . . if you ignored the inconveniences, Thatch, the drunken brawls with knives.

Maybe I would stay.

Make such a decision on the very worst night of all? I was getting like Madge already!

8. The Cook Stays

Bill came in from work early. He slammed his gloves on a kitchen chair. "Damn! We're moving."

"Moving? Well, why the profanity?"

"We're moving to Truckee," he explained. "The boss says they've got another month's rail work over there, and they're going to run in two gangs to rush it through. I thought we'd be going to Colfax next. Now that's sunk."

"What's wrong with Truckee?"

"My dear wife," he said with exaggerated patience, "Colfax is fifty miles in that direction, and only about thirty miles from our house. I figured we could live home and I could drive to work every day, maybe all winter. By spring some other job might open."

"Maybe we won't be at Truckee long," I offered.

"If I know the railroad, a month's rail work means seven or eight weeks. Two months, I betcha. Kay-Kay, I didn't want you to stay in this old outfit any longer than necessary."

Before I could interrupt, Thatch came in and took his jacket out to the tool car as usual. I'd told him he didn't need to hang his things out there, but he'd said simply, "Aw, it makes the place look better." So he'd kept on doing it, and then Bill did too.

Thatch, in other ways, had done a lot to help me. The day after the fight

I'd run out of water and realized Mr. Candy had actually been arrested. So Thatch had seen to it the tanks were filled and kindling in from then on.

Now in the minute he was gone, I said, "Now about this move . . ."

"Later," Bill answered, and stomped off to the bedroom.

I got dinner ready to serve. As we sat down Bill was silent, and Thatch even quieter than usual. They ate like convicts on their last meal, angry at everybody in the world but me. It was obvious my two husbands needed me. Look at them, already mourning the day they'd be batching together again! And it was pretty obvious that if Bill was going to stay on this job, I'd better stay with him.

The gloom was so thick, I made my announcement cautiously. I said, "I think we should vote on whether to keep the cook. I vote YES."

They both stopped eating.

I asked Thatch, "Well, do you think we should keep the cook?"

Bill interrupted. "Kay, I said we'd . . ."

"I'm asking Thatch. The outfits are moving to Truckee, is that right?"

"Guess so," Thatch answered.

"Do you think I should go along?"

"I donno."

"You're just afraid to say! Bill's not your boss now. What do you think?"

Thatch wouldn't say, but there was no doubt about his opinion. Bill fretted and fumed and said there was a lot to consider but actually he didn't want to discuss it with Thatch there. So we discussed it in bed that night in monotones, which probably disturbed our star boarder even more.

"Kay, how come you changed your mind?"

"I didn't change it. I never made it up."

He pulled me close to him. I thought, now this has got more to do with it, you Apache! If you'd put your arms around me every hour on the hour I'd go through anything.

"We could try it for a few months," he whispered. "By then maybe another job will open up. But what if you get pregnant, here in this baggage? Those things happen."

"Don't worry," I said with absolute certainty. In the next room Thatch stirred on his cot. Bill was silent, figuring that one out.

"At least we'll be in a town," he offered.

I thought he'd gone to sleep. "That will help," I agreed. "Could we fix up the outfit a little?"

"Sure. Paint the kitchen, clean things up." He turned over on one elbow, in the dark. "Say, why couldn't we bring some of our things up here, like the sofa and the overstuffed chair, the bureau?"

"What about our house?"

"Give it up. Vacate."

Oh, no! If we kept the house there would always be something solid to go back to . . . but we'd be paying rent and not using it. That was foolish when you thought about it. "Maybe we could keep the house for a little while," I suggested.

"It's just not practical," he insisted. "Let me think about this, got to make some plans."

"Can't they wait until morning?"

"Look, tomorrow is Wednesday. If we shipped our stuff up on the local Thursday they could unload it right here alongside the outfit car, with no problem. If we wait until the outfits are in Truckee we may be off in the yards somewhere and have to handle the stuff a couple of times." He thought it over for a minute, then, "Why couldn't you go down early tomorrow, close up the house, and arrange to ship the things up here?"

"Dear, I don't know if I could handle all that."

"Sure you can if you get an early start. You can stay overnight with Dad and Tillie and drive back Thursday."

Bill was up an hour early to start breakfast. Leaving Thatch to fix his own, we scrambled down the trail to the Buick. Bill scraped the frost from the windshield and started the motor while the fir trees stood shivering in the early light of dawn. When I was behind the wheel he patted my arm. "Kay-Kay, you look real cute when you get up early!" I wondered if I looked that way because I was about to abandon the world of normal people who lived in houses.

"Now don't worry," he insisted. "Just find a transfer company in Roseville and tell them the deal. At the freight office be sure to tell the agent it is an employee's household goods, or they'll want them crated."

"You explained all that."

"And remember, don't ship the refrigerator." He was very firm about that. "Store it at Letterman's for the time being."

On the highway a refrain kept running through my mind: If Madge can do it, I can. As towns came along and the sun warmed up to its job, enthusiasm began to seep in. How many young couples get a chance to pioneer in an outfit car? If we got the old thing furnished comfortably it might be a unique kind of existence. 'Existence' was the wrong word; I reminded myself not to use it again.

It is easy to argue with yourself if you know beforehand what the outcome is going to be. I thought I was making an unbiased decision all by myself. Actually it was the old biological fact of being in love; a condition that gets more women into more predicaments.

In Roseville I located a transfer concern and told the driver the best way to find the place was to follow me. When I drove into the yard with the truck tagging behind, Mrs. L. almost fell on her face.

"Kay! You're not moving away? Without any warning at all?"

She fretted while I tried to convince her it was true, that I really had to hurry to get our things to the freight station that afternoon. "But I might stay with you folks tonight and drive back in the morning."

"Of course you must." As if that would give her an opportunity to change my mind. "You are going to live in a railroad car up in the mountains? Now Kay, you should think it over first."

Our little house was covered with vines, the lawn neatly cut, but it looked forlorn, as if the flowers had tried to close the place because the people who lived there were gone. Gritting my teeth, I started directing the men what to take. The chair, sofa and chest of drawers were the main things. Clothes and dishes could go in the Buick. The refrigerator . . . Bill said to leave it . . . Why? Madge had hers in the outfit. Ours wasn't even paid for and Bill wanted to store it, for no telling how long.

"You can load the refrigerator, too," I told them.

I followed the truck back to Roseville, where I had to argue with the freight agent about shipping them uncrated just as Bill had anticipated. He didn't want to bother with an employee's household goods or argue with employee's wives who didn't know all the answers, and he didn't even like the sound of Cisco. But he took the stuff and I drove back to Lettermans.

At dinner Dad was not only interested that Bill had taken his job seriously and wanted me to move up there, he was all for the idea. "Little discomfort is good for youngsters," he declared. He acted as if a young wife moving into an antiquated baggage car was an everyday occurrence.

But I felt he had lifted a load from my shoulders.

Next morning I ate breakfast with the folks, said goodbye and headed the Buick toward the distant mountains. The car was loaded with my dishes and linens, the rest of our bedding, Bucky the canary — Tillie said he had been very lonesome for us — and a potted geranium. That was a present from Mrs. L. "to brighten up those awful surroundings." I turned onto the highway wondering if the geranium would survive the trip and if Bucky would die of fright when a freight train thundered by the outfit.

Roseville was the first stop, to load up with groceries and especially vegetables; we would have a refrigerator now! And to get a pair of rough shoes to tramp up and down that trail. The clerk at the store thought I was slightly nuts because I picked a pair of boy's size work shoes. I explained I was going camping in some very rough mountains. I didn't say permanently.

The highway was hot and crowded, Bucky panting in his cage on the seat beside me, but the geranium was doing nicely, wedged against the door on the floor. It would put some color in the old baggage car at that, and remind me of Mrs. Letterman and our little house. Was the honeymoon cottage a thing of the past? I bit my lip and drove on.

At the lonely but quiet, cool parking place at Cisco, I unpacked the hiking shoes first. They fit fine, and I hardly felt the rocks as I scrambled up the trail with Bucky and the geranium. The camp cars were still there, so were the tracks and the mountains, but all was not serene.

My husband, with his helper, was standing hands-on-hips glaring at our shiny refrigerator standing in the gravel beside the main line, along with the chair and sofa, floor lamp, and assorted boxes. I asked, "Dear, what's the matter?"

He swung around, and without kissing me or saying hello, said, "Why did you ship the . . . you didn't bring that worthless canary too!"

"Well, I couldn't leave him; he's a wedding present."

My husband took off his gloves and slammed them down on the ties. "First tell me why you shipped the refrigerator."

"I thought it was silly to store it away and go on making payments. Madge has one. Why can't we?"

He shook his head. "I should have explained. Madge's has been converted to an icebox. They drilled a hole in it for the purpose, because most of the time we can't hook to any line with enough power to run a motor like that."

"But . . ."

"Their's is old. If it got damaged the loss wouldn't be serious. Ours is brand new and I'm not going to drill a hole in it for ice."

I didn't say any more, but Bill knew that hopeless as the situation might be, refrigerator, wife, and canary, he was stuck with all three. He and Thatch heaved and pulled until they got the gleaming box into our dingy kitchen. It made the whole outfit car look more ancient than ever. He grumbled about having to bolt it solid some way, but better get the other things first.

"Maybe in Truckee we'll have enough power to run it," I offered.

Finally he showed some sympathy. "For your sake, I hope so."

Dinner was on the stove. Bucky was bouncing in his cage in the 'living room' which now looked quite homey with the chair and sofa. The chair had been placed between the stove and Thatch's cot, the sofa and lamp stood against the opposite wall, slightly crowding Bill's desk. Bill and Thatch had lugged all the dishes and groceries up the trail. The potted geranium reposed temporarily in the middle of the kitchen table.

I heard the distant pounding of an approaching freight. "Oh, Bill, do you think it will scare Bucky?"

"I hope it scares the feathers right off his tail," Bill said in his towel.

Thatch stopped, soap on his face. "Gee, do you think so? I kinda like canaries."

I went to the living room doorway. Bucky was getting excited. The roar drew closer, windows began to rattle. Bucky hopped onto his perch and burst into song. NOISE! He loved it. He sang at the top of his shrill voice as the giant Mallet outside rocked his cage. We all stood in the room and gaped.

"I told you he was crazy," Bill shouted.

Thatch stood beside the cage grinning at a new friend. I went back to my cookstove, mumbling, "Maybe he is crazy . . . and knows he's among friends."

Bucky sang until the last helper engine was out of hearing. And from then on he always announced gleefully that a train was coming.

9. Stock Corral Five

The day awoke like any other, but there all similarity ended.

Thatch ate unhurriedly and had his leisurely cigarette, but Bill hardly tasted his breakfast. "The work train should be here around ten," he predicted. "You'd better wait until you actually see the cars moving out; anything can happen. Thatch, start checking the stuff in the tool car. And, Kay when you get to Truckee..."

"I just wait 'til the outfits get there," I added. "When they are through switching, I can go in. You said all that."

"I know, but it's your first move and I don't want you to worry. Well, we got a lot to do. You can help by doing the dishes right away and put them in the cupboard. Shove a few towels between the stacks."

He went off into the tool car, pulling on his jacket, and the excitement began to affect me. I did the dishes in about ten minutes and then started putting things away, like Madge would. I heard Bill and Thatch banging around in the tool car, then the lights went out. Next someone was knocking on my 'back' door. It was Bill. "Got any further need for the dreamhouse?"

"Well, for goodness sake . . . I might."

"Borrow Nichols. O.K. Thatch," he said like a construction boss. Right before my eyes they tipped the dreamhouse over, started walking toward the tool car with it and shoved it bodily into the wide side door.

"I thought it would be heavy," I said. "You boys sure know how to handle your privies."

Thatch grinned. "Maybe we learned it when we were kids."

"Bill, what happened to the lights?"

"I took the wires down. Did you think we were just plugged into the track or something?"

I hadn't thought about it at all. The only reason I could remember for lights going out was when a fuse was blown. But sure enough, Thatch came along pulling a long tangled string of wire which he coiled up on the floor in the tool car. Then he got a shovel and climbed out of the car with it.

"Do you have to dig us out or something, Thatch?" I asked.

He pointed to where the dreamhouse had stood. "Gotta fill up the hole."

Nothing like a straightforward answer. I went back to my work. Bill was in the kitchen nailing a long board across the cupboard doors. "Now what?"

"Liable to have dishes all over the floor," he explained. "I'll put some hasps on these doors some day. Put your coffee pot on the floor in the corner."

"I will not put it on the floor! I'll take it with me in the Buick."

"All right, and take that fool canary, too. He'll beat his brains out if we leave him in here."

"Oh, I'd better take my geranium plant," I added.

"For gosh sake, you can't carry all that stuff down the trail." He went to the door and hollered, "C'mere, Thatch. Take this precious pot and this prize geranium down to the Buick."

"Wait," I cried, "I haven't emptied the grounds."

"And empty the grounds on your way!"

Suddenly the rush was over and I was sitting in Madge's kitchen with my coat on and Bucky's cage beside me on a chair. The boys had shooed me out, boosted in the steps, locked the doors, and went puttering off on their motor car. Now all I had to do was sit and wait. At least I heard Sally's Other Husband after all.

Madge was in a griping mood. Roscoe had decided again this morning he was fed up with outfit cars. There was a job open for bid and he wanted to settle down and have a house.

"On the San Joaquin Division," Madge declared. "Right in the heat and traffic. No fishing." She filled my coffee cup again. "I told him flat, nothing doing. I'll tell him when a bid suits me."

I tried to change the subject. "I wish you were moving to Truckee, too."

"Do ya? Truckee's not bad. Well, I told Roscoe if he . . ."

It was like changing a river. "I mean it," I said. "You've been real nice, helping me with everything."

"Ah, kid, you feel bad, don't ya?" she said. "You're sweet, You'll hear from me, and you'll always know where we are. It ain't like you had a system job."

"I guess neighbors come and go if you live in outfits."

"Hell, no!" she argued. "You never lose track of them. You always know where they are and what they're doing, via the grapevine. Maybe two months, or two years later, you find yourself right next door again. Hey, I think I hear your work train." She popped her head out the door. "No, it's the local stopping. Well, paint me green and call me Irish — if it isn't 'Sailor' Reagan!"

A caboose had halted opposite her door and a spry, gray-headed man in striped overalls was crossing the tracks. He wore a striped cap with the brim turned up rakishly and held a pipe clamped in a face that was Irish from the grin to the cherry complexion. He was all of sixty, portly, but his step had the vigor of a once handsome stud horse.

"Belay me!" he cried. "If it isn't my old girl-friend."

Madge went down the steps and they went into each other's arms. It dawned on me that she was Irish, too. Mr. Reagan, completely ignoring the railroad, hugged her and pinched her arm affectionately.

"I missed ya, Nichols," he declared. "Lord, how I missed ya. Say, is that husband of yours anywhere around?"

"You know he isn't, you old windbag."

"Good! Now's our chance, huh?"

"Why, Sailor, I just believe you would!"

He laughed roguishly, showing a mouthful of tobacco-stained teeth, and used the opportunity to pat her arm a little too much. "Too bad I got a train waitin', huh? But say, what I stopped for, you know a lady named Fisher?"

"She's standing right there on the steps staring at you."

"Scuttle me," he announced. "Good thing I didn't say anything about that fine husband of hers." When I stepped down he gave me the arm pinching treatment. "I'm glad to make your acquaintance, Miz Fisher. I'm back on this run after a couple of years, so I'll see a lot of you. But what I stopped for; that husband of yours flagged me down up the line and told me to tell you your outfits aren't going until tomorrow."

"Not going! Well, I like that."

"I'm sorry." He laughed his sympathy. "You just can't depend on work trains, Miz Fisher. Well, I'm sure glad to meet ya." He bounced off across the track, waving a haphazard signal to his engine. The train went chomping away.

"That," Madge said, "was Sailor Reagan, the biggest blowhard on the pike."

I wasn't listening. "What'll I do? We aren't going."

This was something you could expect anytime, she explained. She went back to the 713 with me. I was able to swing myself up the ladder after two tries, but she had to help me slide the steps out. Then I realized I couldn't even open the cupboard doors. Madge surveyed the heavy board Bill had nailed across them.

"Got a hammer?" she asked. We found one but it wouldn't budge the nails. Unperturbed, she went out to the tool car, came back with a big railroad pick and calmly ripped the board off. "You gotta be self-sufficient, kid," she laughed.

When the boys came home I had dinner cooking. Quite blindly, they didn't even ask how I got the steps out, or the cupboard doors open. They strung out the electric wires again, but decided to 'borrow' the Nichols dreamhouse for one night.

Next morning we went through the whole procedure again; pull in the wires, stow everything away, nail up the cupboards, boost the steps in, lock all the doors. Bill went to the phone shanty to make sure the work train would actually show up this time.

"Be here about nine," he said when he came back. "Wish I could stay until they get here. Now, Kay, wait for me at the station in Truckee if you have any trouble." So I went over to Madge's and sat with my coat on and sipped coffee, watching Bucky in his cage. Twice, as we waited, I thought I heard the work train but Madge guessed correctly they were through freights.

About ten we heard something like escaping steam above the sound of the radio. "Hey, they're here!" Madge announced. We looked out and found just an engine and caboose standing on the main track. Madge unplugged her radio and laid it in the overstuffed chair, then went into the bedroom and took down her mirror.

"They're got to move ours out to reach yours," she explained. "Come on, we'll watch from outside." We met a brakeman walking along with a stick in his hand. Madge stopped him. "My light wires are plugged in right there on the end of the car. Now I want these four cars right back where they are now. Understand?"

A tall rangy man stepped down from the caboose. Instead of the usual overalls he wore black wool trousers, black vest and a short loose coat but the badge of a railroader, the heavy watch chain, crossed his vest. "What's the trouble here?" he demanded. "I'm the conductor."

"I want these four cars spotted right where they are now," Madge told him belligerently.

He turned away without answering and looked impatiently along the cars. Then with a contemptuous glance at my birdcage, he walked off. The brakeman was now using his stick to manipulate the brake wheel on top of Madge's car. He scurried expertly down the iron ladder and pulled her steps away, letting them drop to the ground.

They left their caboose by itself on the mainline and backed the engine into the spur track. Then with mysterious sign language they began connecting the long string of cars together. There was much standing still and noise from the engine. When the coupling wouldn't work a brakeman would hold out his fist and waggle one thumb in the air, then he'd hold both arms outstretched and rock back and forth. The cars would wham together with a lurch, the tin stovepipes vibrating.

"How can these old cars stand such treatment?" I wondered.

"Some of 'em have been standing it for forty years," Madge said. "The crews sure hate outfits. They call them 'soft bellies'." The brakeman seemed merely disinterested but the tall conductor stood to one side with his chin stuck out sourly. "Kay, that's Bert Slate. He's a brother to that constable who was here the other night. They're both ornery cusses."

I had imagined some shouting romantically, "All aboard!" as the train departed but this was an agonizingly slow process. There was more backing and pulling, then finally one brakeman waved a circle with his stick and the engine moved ahead . . . for two feet. Steam hissed, the cars groaned, nothing happened. Suddenly there was a crashing exhaust from the engine and its wheels spun crazily on the rails. Mr. Slate cursed. More hissing and the cars moved ever so slightly.

With its last ounce of strength the engine coaxed the cars into motion, dragging them slowly up the track. Cooky unexpectedly waved to us from his cook car. The rusty spur was left with piles of ashes, assorted cans, and Madge's dreamhouse.

Then the whole train backed toward us on the main track until it nudged the caboose. More signals; the engine moved ahead pulling only Madge's four cars. It came slowly into the spur track and stopped with each one in the exact spot it had been before.

"Humph," Madge declared, "they can do it if they want to!"

Out the engine went again onto the main track, back toward us until it bumped our ragged tool car. Everybody waited a while, the young fireman giving us the once over. There was a long urgent whistle, sounds of air in the brake system, two more blasts on the whistle. The crew strolled toward the caboose, one of them waving his stick over his head. The engineer used his whistle to say "Wowt, wowt". The painful process of snorting, slipping and jerking began again. The long string of outfits lurched, as if it were difficult to all move at the same time but finally, to the occasional slap of flat wheels, they began to resemble a moving train.

Norden, where the houses are connected to each other and to the snowsheds by wooden tunnels. *(Walter Keck collection)*

"They are off in a cloud of soot," I said.

"And no telling when they'll arrive," Madge laughed. "Come in and have some coffee. You got lots of time."

The highway curved beautifully on its way through the craggy hills. Ahead, the peaks of the Sierra Nevada rose like a great stone barricade across the top of the world. Once I pulled up behind a large truck and followed it for several miles before I could pass. I passed some ski lodges. Then below the highway I saw a long row of railroad houses, all a drab yellow color with dull green roofs. They were connected together by wooden tunnels and they in turn connected to an array of massive black wooden structures that reached as far as the eye could see. This must be Norden and the famous snowsheds. What a forbidding place. I hoped the outfit cars would never be parked there.

A sign said 7000 feet and then I was met by a spectacular view, a panorama of mountains, Donner Lake far below, and the highway twisting downward like a rope thrown against the cliffs. I shifted the Buick into second gear. There was one sharp curve after another and I caught up with another truck inching its way downgrade. Eventually the road leveled out and skimmed along that beautiful blue lake.

Truckee was a smudge in all this beauty, a collection of dingy buildings and houses lying like a swirl of driftwood among the surrounding mountains. At the east end of town I could see a dozen yard tracks, repair shops with plumes of white steam coming from pipes stuck through metal roofs. A pall of brown smoke lay over the town.

The main street was entirely taken up on the right side by the railroad, a large yellowish hotel, and the station. On the left a chain of mix-matched

"Truckee was a smudge in all this beauty."　　　　　　　*(Walter Keck collection)*

buildings looked onto a dusty street crowded with parked automobiles. There seemed to be two grocery stores, one at each end of the block as if they'd been added reluctantly to the string of bars and sporting goods stores.

Walking along the street I noticed a movie theatre. Dust and papers had collected at the entrance. A sign in the cashier's booth said Saturday, Sunday and Wednesday Only, the marquee announced; Now Showing, Dorothy Lamour in South Seas & News. Then I found a variety store and for me, Truckee officially became a town.

Shopping in the best looking of the two grocery stores I promptly learned that prices rise with the altitude hereabouts. A fresh young clerk was at the register. "Nice to see a new face," he leered. "Find everything you want?"

"Yes, and I didn't miss your prices," I told him.

He carried the things out to the car, scaring poor Bucky. "We deliver, you know. You can phone in your order."

Wouldn't he be surprised if I said, "Okay, deliver these to Baggage Car 713 on track so-and-so."

I walked across to the station and in the door marked TICKETS — WESTERN UNION. There were the usual benches, doors lettered MEN, WOMEN, the steam radiators. But I'd expected tile floors; these were rough oiled boards with a musty odor. Behind a screened window sat the ticket agent, complete with eyeshade and clicking telegraph instruments, reading a newspaper. He was thin, gray-headed, with pince-nez glasses and a stringy tie.

I said, "Say, I'd like to find out when my train will get here."

He got up and came to the window. "Which way you going, lady?"

"I'm not going anywhere."

Truckee. The buildings, all on one side of the street, faced the railroad.
(From a postcard)

He looked bored. "You meeting somebody? What train?"

"The work train with my outfit car, the 713."

"Outfit cars are none of my business." He turned away. I thought, Madge would tell him off!

"Well, whose business is it?" I persisted.

"Which work train, lady? Where you moving from?"

"Cisco."

"Slate's train. Can't tell when he'll get in."

"Well, can you tell me where they'll put my outfit car?"

He looked disgusted. "Ask Hennesy, the yardmaster."

"Thanks very much. Where do I find the yardmaster?"

He nervously shuffled a pad of telegram blanks. "Just go outside and wait, lady. The first person you see hurrying will be him."

I walked out the door marked TO TRAINS, wondering if he treated passengers that way. Well, if I were a passenger I wouldn't ride on his darned railroad.

The air was cold, a cloudy wind driving bits of paper along the rough pavement and around the wheels of the baggage trucks. I sat on a bench and looked for someone hurrying. Not a soul in sight. Across the multiple tracks were some railroad houses, further on several small sheds and a row of poplar trees. Rising between the mountains in the distance was a cloud of black smoke. Yes, there was some sign of life.

A Mallet engine was now chuffing up one of the tracks with a man riding on the footstep. It rattled through the switches toward me and stopped. The man jumped off and ran ahead to throw a switch. The engine moved ahead, he threw the switch again, the engine went backing away without him. He came hurrying toward the station. That, I decided, must be Mr. Hennesy.

"Pardon me, are you the yardmaster?"

He was a short, fatherly man with a brown suitcoat over his striped overalls, the usual watch chain and black hat. He said pleasantly, "Yes'm, I'm him."

"Well, can you tell me when the work train will be here and where they will put my outfits?"

He strode to the telegraph office, pushed open a window and hollered, "Where's Slate?"

"Just hit the bug," the agent said sourly.

"They'll be here pretty quick, Ma'am." He pulled a paper from his pocket. "Fisher, two cars. Well, Missus Fisher, where to put you is a problem. Not room up here in this end of town."

"Why, there are lots of tracks," I declared, trying to sound like Madge. "What about that one over by those trees?"

"Maybe it doesn't look it but that's our busiest siding. All these tracks are busy, can't be blocking them with outfits. Best I can do is Corral Track Five. Drive down Main and take that street that crosses the tracks, see it there?" He pointed. "Turn left and follow that road for about a mile and a half."

"A mile and a half!" I cried. "I thought we'd be right in town."

He shrugged. "They don't build railroads for outfit cars, Missus Fisher. Lot of outfits down there. You'll be on the far end. But I promise to move you up here in town the first spot I get."

An engine came clanking downgrade toward the station pulling just our outfits and a caboose. Mr. Hennesy held up one hand with five fingers spread wide. Conductor Slate on the caboose steps replied with the same gesture and the short train rattled on past. The yardmaster hurried off to the cloud of black smoke which had turned into a freight train and I was left standing there.

So this was how Madge developed her tough attitude. This was the respect you got when you lived in an outfit car.

Dejectedly I went back to the Buick. 'Turn left after you cross the tracks'. The street from there on became a rough curbless lane with railroad houses on one side and shacks on the other. After a block it degenerated into a path.

I wound through rocky dry grass country, sometimes close to the tracks, sometimes losing them. There were murky puddles and cow dabs to break the monotony. When I thought I must have gone two miles I saw a woman ahead walking. She had on a loose black coat, low shoes and no stockings. She kept walking, carrying a shopping bag of groceries and a package, until I had to stop for her.

"Is this the road to the corral track?" I called out.

She had brown sticky hair, a tired pasty-white face on which she had painted a red mouth. She stood as if her back ached. "That's where I'm goin'," she said, dragging on a cigarette, then dropping it to crush it out. "You live in a outfit?"

"Yes. Can I give you a lift?"

"Sure thing." She went around the car and got in, holding the package on her lap. "Thanks, honey. Sure nice car you got." She felt the upholstery.

"It's several years old," I said. "Did you walk all the way?"

"My ole man won't allow me to drive." She felt the seat. "Sure nice car, honey. What outfit you in?"

"Signal department. My husband is Bill Fisher." As I spoke she lit another cigarette, holding it in the middle of her mouth. We climbed a short rise and came in view of a maze of empty stock corrals. Alongside them was a half-mile string of outfit cars. It looked like a long circus train with coaches, boxcars, tanks, loaded flat cars, some recently painted, some sagging, some with washing strung across open spaces.

"Fisher? Don't know him," she said without removing her cigarette. "If you just come in you'll be way down next to me."

Next to her? "How long have you been here?" I asked.

"Us? All summer. My ole man is a extra gang foreman, Terroli. Know him?" The Buick lurched in a chuck hole and she grabbed the package in her lap. "C'mere, baby. Half gallon of wine," Mrs. Terroli explained. "My ole man and me like to keep some around. Don't suppose you take any?"

Apparently not expecting an answer, she sat staring at the road, sucking on her cigarette and holding the wine tightly now. We rocked and splashed along the corrals, then the road ended abruptly. Half a dozen automobiles of mixed ages were parked facing the track, and there stood the 713 and 787!

"Guess them's your outfits," Mrs. Terroli said. "Thanks for the ride."

I sat in the Buick watching her walk jerkily up the weed-grown track along the corrals. She passed the first three cars which looked like tool cars and climbed the steps of a battered coach. My own high reddish baggage car stood waiting for me to take over. Why did outfits have to be so old . . . so ragged . . . and such an awful mud red? Why did they have to be in such ungodly places, alongside such people? I had thought Madge was typical of other outfit families. Now I wondered if Mrs. Terroli was.

"Well, Bucky, I guess we're home on Corral Track Five." I opened the door. The wind met me, heavy with a pungent aroma. "Oh no!"

Like a constant tradewind, the aroma was inescapable.

Like a constant tradewind, it was inescapable. I stood there transfixed by the miracle of stale cow manure. Chin up, Kay-Kay. Anyone could enjoy a bottle of Chanel No. 5 but how many could say they'd lived on Corral Number Five? "For two cents," I said to Bucky, ". . . for two measly cents I'd go out and get a hotel room."

Bucky didn't have two cents. Probably it was lucky he didn't; anything might have happened. I gritted my teeth, walked over and grasped the iron ladder of my home on rails and did a Madge Nichols leap, making it on the first try but ripping my coat sleeve in the process. I crawled into the baggage car and proceeded to struggle with the steps until I got the heavy things out, at the cost of a kinked back. Then I carried Bucky, the geranium, coffee pot, and groceries inside, twice tripping over the track between the outfit and the Buick. Next I picked up the teakettle, which was upside down on the floor, mopped up the spilled water, remembering not to leave it on the stove next time, shut the oven door, took the ashpan out of the stove, went out to dump it and had the wind blow the ashes back in my face.

I was in a bad mood when I heard a motorcar coming.

It came clattering up the weedy track but it wasn't Bill and Thatch. As it went by, two men on it gawked. Next, a large motorcar with four or five trailers of men came by, and another. Apparently the residents of Corral

Number Five were coming home. Last, but not least, Bill and Thatch came ticking along, stopped and pulled their car off into the gravel.

"Hiya, wife," my husband greeted happily. "See you got here." He clumped up the steps, trying them for solidness. "Who put the steps out for you?"

I glared at him.

"You did?" He hugged me with one arm, actually hugged me right in front of Thatch. "Kay-Kay, you'll make a railroader yet." In his crude Apachian way he appreciated me, I guess.

I said, "Why can't they put us on another track? This is awful."

He shook his head. "Yardmaster said he'd move us the first chance. We'll have to use kerosene lamps here; no power connection within half a mile."

"Coal oil lamps?" So that's why those tin lamps were fastened to the walls. "What about my radio and refrigerator?"

"No radio," he shrugged, "and of course no refrigerator."

So this was Truckee. I looked at the steak I'd bought to celebrate being in a town . . . on a corral track with oil lamps. When I peered out a while later, the boys were prodding the ground with a crowbar. "What are you looking for?" I called. "Dinner is almost ready."

"Must have been outfits here all summer. No spot for the dreamhouse."

I thought, fine . . . let's just do without!

10. Shop Track One

Cattle, hundreds of them!

We'd been in Truckee six weeks and I was just learning what those stock corrals were for. Bill explained that the cattle grazed in the high mountain meadows in summer. Now they were being shipped to lower elevations.

"Shore reminds me of home," Thatch observed, standing in the doorway watching the winter sun go down through the cloud of dust.

All night they'd bawled their collective protest at being penned up, and all day a switch engine had snorted back and forth with noisy, crowded loads of them to a background of yelling cowboys driving in more. The nervous cows stomped continually in the open cars, kicking up a fine aromatic dust and dropping their fresh splattering gobs through the slatted sides. Now, with the stench of engine smoke still in my kitchen and the bawling in the corrals getting in tune for another long night, I wished Thatch would indeed go home and take his smelly four-footed friends with him.

In those six weeks I'd definitely lost my rose-colored glasses. I'd found out more about railroads, people, outfits, and how to get gray hair than I thought possible. I'd learned the hard way how to fill, clean, trim, and read by coal oil lamps, and how to load a drunk into an automobile. I learned more about living with husbands, too, and saw Thatcher Kelly lose his halo and gain a new one virtually all in one breath.

Dora Terroli was a different experience, the lasting kind. She came to visit me the first morning, and every blessed morning thereafter. Her faded dress with no bra and probably no pants under it, grew dirtier with each passing day. None of my ashtrays were big enough, so when the butts began spilling onto my kitchen table I'd throw the mess out onto the tracks and she'd start refilling again.

"You sure got a nice man, honey." She could start and end with that comment every day. "Now my ole man, he won't take me out or buy me nothin'. He won't fix nothin' neither."

Her 'ole man' was a greasy, dark, egotistical person who smoked vicious curled cigars and wore overalls Sundays, holidays, and overtime. He started clean on Saturday night and wore everything until the next Saturday, rain or shine, dirty or not. He did 'take her out' though. This amounted to driving uptown in their dented muddy car and spending the evening lolling over a bar. They were a standard fixture in town every Saturday night, and in between if there was any event such as payday.

When the car wouldn't run they walked. Coming along the rutted road after a movie, our headlights would pick them out walking Indian style with him in the lead and one or both toting a wine jug on one finger. "Don't pick them up, Bill," I said the first time.

"Heck no. We'd never get rid of them."

Bill tried to fix their car but gave up. He said it hadn't been greased or washed since the day it was manufactured. The windows looked it, too. Apparently neither of them had ever been anywhere, ever read a paper or had any friends. Like the outfit cars they lived in, being twenty or thirty years behind times made no difference at all.

Dora's world and therefore her conversation revolved around her 'ole man', the railroad, the weather last week, last year, and the year before that. It grew so tiresome I got so I could go on with my work and never hear her. She liked me because I listened and didn't condemn her, and I realized sadly that she envied me. Once pathetically she hit the nail on the head. "My trouble, honey, is I never had no bringin' up nor no school housin'."

Just when I thought one more visit from Dora would be too much, she quit coming. Then I worried, and that was a mistake.

It was three days after payday and I was shopping in town, enjoying the infrequent sunshine, and had just met Conductor Reagan on the street. He remembered me instantly and chattered about 'Miz Nichols', who had moved to some location I couldn't recall, and then went off in his peppy way . . .

"Hey, Kay. Hey honey, it's me!" Dora was staggering from post to post.

She fell on me with reeking breath and clinging arms. Her eyes were bloodshot under the hair hanging in her face, the make-up had caked, the red mouth a smeared blob of crimson. She smelled of stale cigarette smoke, spilled liquor and sweat. "Y're the onlifren I got. Will ya take me 'ome? I'm sick." She stood swaying, hanging onto me, lips too numb to form words.

People were walking around us staring. "Please try to stand up, Dora. My car is right down here. Come on."

"Aw righ'." She stood with an exaggerated expression of pleading. "An' I 'ppreciate it. I 'ppreciate all my frens. Tell ya what, 'll buy ya a drink. Here's place where they know me."

"No!" I declared. "I don't want a drink. I'm in a hurry."

She sensed I might get away, her arm clasped my neck again. "Honey, I gotta have a drink I'm so sick. We'll have a li'l one together."

With everyone watching, a street scene was the worst of two evils so I let her drag me into the dim bar. The bartender and several customers appraised us mercilessly. "Now, Dora," I told her, "I've got to go. I haven't time for a drink. If you want to come along . . ."

"One li'l drink . . . o' good stuff." She leered at the bartender, clawing toward a stool. "Give her . . . my fren a Tom Collins and me a strayshot. Collins awrigh', honey?"

"Really, I don't want anything. I'm going now."

The bartender said, "You had about enough, Mrs. Terroli."

"Hell with you!" she told him. "Ya think I'm drunk, doncha? Well, I'm not. I'm sick."

"Just the same . . ."

"I said I'm sick. She's my fren and she's takin' me 'ome, righ'? But firs' we gotta have a drink."

He surveyed us coldly and began to mix a drink. Dora took a cigarette from a crushed pack in the pocket of her dress and held it in the center of her mouth. The dress was torn and stained, dirty circles outlined her breasts where grimy hands had explored. I hated her but I felt sorry for her.

"Y're the only fren I got, honey," she said again. Her drink was on the bar but she made no move to pick it up. "I been drunk for thrrree days. My ole man came after me once but I ran off from him. I know what he wan's, the bas'ard. Tha's all he wan's, too."

Disgust sickened me. I finally sipped the drink on the promise we'd leave then and there. She had only a few nickels so I paid. She half-walked a meandering route to the Buick, but was unable to get in. Burning with embarrassment, I helped her crawl into the seat, but before I could start the motor she opened the door again.

"Wait, honey. That bar, that's where I left it. Be righ' back."

Before I could stop her, she was out of the car and staggering across the sidewalk. Remembering she had no purse, I waited. Several minutes passed while I debated whether to drive away or go looking for her.

She was sitting at the bar with some seedy character fondling the dirty circles on her dress, but she saw me come in . . . and the door swing shut as I went out. "Honey, I'm sorrry." She crawled sorrowfully into the seat as I held the clutch down.

I didn't speak as we crept along the rutted road but she made up for the silence. "Ya don' like me, do ya? An' I don' blame ya. I'm no goddam good." She sat staring straight ahead, tears soaking into the thick white powder on her face. "I used to think I was somebody. Hell, I wasn' foolin' anybody but my own damn self. Ya know what I was, honey? I was the bes' damn whore ever worked this town, and I never took a drink, believe me."

I believed her. The twisting lane was longer than it ever had been. She opened the door before I shut off the motor and went staggering off toward her coach.

I carried the groceries inside, then sat down on a kitchen chair with my coat on and stared out the open door.

What was I doing in this world of stock corrals, Dora Terrolis, coal stoves, oil lamps and switch engines? There were no answers and, for the moment, no solution.

Roy Ramgaw was the signal maintainer in Truckee. Bill soon got to know Roy and thought we both should get acquainted with him and his wife, Emma, because Bill wanted me to see what it was like to have a maintainer's job, the thing we were supposed to be working toward.

Roy had a 'district', a section of railroad over which he traveled by motor-car, caring for all the block signal equipment, crossing wigwags, wayside telephones, slide warning devices and the pole line. They lived rent free in a 'company' house across from the station. Outside, it was the standard drab railroad color with a pathetic, struggling lawn and a half-dozen tracks for view. Inside it had old-fashioned high ceilings, tongue-and-groove walls, tall narrow windows, and a single light fixture hanging in the center of each room. But it did have five rooms furnished in a neat homey way, and a real honest-to-goodness bathroom. Not a gleaming tile affair; the tub had legs under it and the faucets were spring type, but it was warm, cheerful and private!

"Tell me," I said the first evening we visited them, "did you folks live in our outfit?" I remembered 'R. Ramgaw' on the old reports on Bill's desk.

"Oh, yes," Emma replied in her peculiar soft voice. "I lived in it until two years ago. Then they added two helpers and I had to move out." She was thin and tall with large blue eyes, light hair, and beautiful teeth. She smiled as if she really felt it but her smile, like her voice, was retiring, modest, as if anything she touched might break.

The signal maintainer's house in Truckee.   *(Robert DelCarlo collection)*

"How did you ever stand it? Didn't you get lonesome?"

"Oh my, yes," she said. "Of course you have a helper with you. Roy and I were alone most of the time. And you won't be isolated the way we were. Roy worried about me."

Roy worried was an understatement; he fretted continually. At first glance he might be a farmer, dry sense of humor, more at home in overalls talking over a backyard fence. I could imagine him being uncomfortable in a suit. Easily ten years older than she, with gray hair beginning where his glasses creased his temples, railroads, particularly block signals, were his life. He and Bill settled down to talking about their work like a couple of old women. But if Emma made a move he was ready to do whatever it was for her.

"Oh now, Roy, I can do it," she'd say, but her voice was so undemanding he'd go right on against her protests. Later, when we became better acquainted, she confided, "He acts that way because I had a miscarriage once. He swears it was caused by my climbing down from the outfit when the steps weren't in place, but I don't think it was." She spoke as if it were so long ago. I was mixed up.

"Kay, an odd thing happened one time," she related. "I lost my voice."

"You lost your voice?"

"Yes, they were building the new line on the north end. We were miles from nowhere that whole summer, no towns or people except the track gangs. I thought it was Roy's hearing, but it was my own voice getting faint. Finally it quit altogether. He had to take me to a doctor, on the train, mind you."

"For goodness sake, what was wrong?"

She looked to see if the men were listening. "I'm embarrassed to tell you, Kay. The doctor said I just wasn't talking enough. He was amazed that it could happen. But I was alone on that lonely spur all day, and when Roy came home he didn't talk much."

"I can't believe it," I exclaimed. "You actually lost your voice because there was no one to talk to?"

"Yes, and I was so embarrassed."

Roy had been tuned in to our talk. "Maybe you think I didn't feel silly, Missus Fisher. The doc said we should fight once in a while, so she'd shout at me. No kidding! Her voice never was the same again."

"Oh, Roy, it got all right."

But it hadn't. I thought, lady, if you ever have to holler for help you'll drown or suffocate before anyone hears you. "Is that all the doctor recommended?" I asked.

"He said to get a dog and talk to it all the time, even sing to it. So we did, but I just couldn't bring myself to sing to Spike."

What a happy state to look forward to, I thought. What other hazards were there in outfit cars? Perhaps I should look up some more former residents.

"We still have Spike," Emma added. "He's six now."

"Six? How long were you in the outfit?" Panic was in my voice.

"Roy had it seven years altogether."

"Bill," I cried, "They had the outfit seven years. Did you hear that?"

Bill said, "I wish you hadn't mentioned it, Emma."

But you won't be in it that long, they hastened to add. Jobs are changing, oldtimers retiring, bids would be opening up now. I couldn't tell if they believed it or not.

The Ramgaws were a big help, though, in making life in Truckee more endurable. They understood what I was going through and were some assurance that I might come through with all my senses; but I'd have to watch for that hazard of losing my voice!

Of course they played pinochle, so I had to learn. Once I grasped the game it became fun, and I could slam down the last trump and holler "Yippee" with the best of them. We often went to the movie with them on Sunday night.

Attending a movie was like an old-fashioned basket social. Everyone collected on the sidewalk before the theatre opened, chatting about the railroad, fishing, deer hunting. The Mexican boys would be there in brown suits and red neckties, their hair shiny with oil, chattering in clicking Spanish. They were very polite. A group of trainmen would be discussing the war in Europe with loud authority, their watch chains flashing on clean striped overalls. But the largest part of the crowd around the glass ticket booth would be kids, all shoving and teasing noisily.

When the picture started the kids would let out a cheer, no matter what came on the screen. The manager would stride down the aisle pushing a wave of temporary silence ahead of him. On his way back the wave of chatter would resume. The sound track would be completely blanked out if a freight was pulling out of the yards. The first engine would stomp by so slowly you could catch a word between each exhaust blast, but when the rear helper engine came along with its throttle 'back against the pin' the roof would rise a couple of feet and drop back. Dorothy Lamour would say, "Oh, Ramon, I lub oo of mu. Tell me at oo ont beev."

I always stopped to see Emma when I drove into town to shop. "Just stopped to enjoy your bathroom," I'd tell her, and she sympathized with me. I resolved that when I had a house again I'd have my own private bathroom.

One day I told her about meeting Madge Nichols. "She's a kick, isn't she," Emma smiled. "They were here this summer. She had a big argument with Dora Terroli."

"That Dora person!" I exclaimed, and related a well-buttered account of my taking Dora home when she was drunk. Then in her soft, kind way Emma set me back on my heels.

"I know Dora is all you say, Kay. Worse, I suppose, if we knew. But I almost feel as if I owe my life to her."

"Really," I wondered. "How do you mean?"

"There was a fire one night. We were in the outfit about where you are now. It started in some tool cars next to us. I guess one had some barrels of gasoline and the fire was out of control in no time. The roof of the 713 had started burning when the Terrolis came home from town. Dora began pounding on our door and hollering."

"She woke you up?"

"We had the shades down and Roy wouldn't answer her; he thought she

83

was just drunk. So Dora threw a rock through the bedroom window, and of course we saw the flames then. Roy flagged a freight train and they used the engine to pull our cars away from the burning ones. Then Roy saved our roof with buckets of water."

I didn't know what to say, but I resolved to treat Dora with as much kindness as I could muster.

We had been in Truckee almost a month when I met Jack and Beverly Wessa, the first couple our age I'd seen. At first I was thrilled to have another girl for a neighbor, and then I was disappointed.

Beverly drove up one windy afternoon in a new car. I saw her walk toward the track with her hands on hips. She was tall and cute in turned up jeans and white sweater. She was wearing glasses and had brown hair cut in bangs.

"Hello," I greeted. "Are you looking for an outfit?"

"Yes, and I see it isn't here yet. Is this corral track five? What a stinking place."

"It isn't so bad when the wind is not blowing. Won't you come in? I'm Kay Fisher."

"Signal department? I've heard of you." She came inside and sat on the sofa. "This is a good idea. I suppose it's some old furniture you had."

I didn't tell her it was all we had. "How did you know about us?"

"Jack is a burro crane operator. Track department. He knows your husband. I'm Beverly."

"How long have you lived in an outfit?"

"Just this summer and I hate it. My folks have a ranch. They don't like my living like this, but Jack thinks we should be together." She injected sarcasm into the words.

I noticed the leather sandals and good nylons, and a diamond ring big enough to make any girl's heart sing. I decided she was spoiled. She was about twenty-three; I wondered if mama had told her to get out and get married.

"You have more room than our boxcar," she observed, "but it sure needs painting, doesn't it?" She got up and looked in the kitchen. She liked the refrigerator but when I told her it was useless, she stared. "You mean there's no chance for lights here? Wait 'til Jack hears that! He's going to trot right up to McKinney's office and get us moved or this chick isn't staying around until dark."

Evidently her husband didn't have any better luck than Bill in getting away from corral tracks. Her outfit arrived late in the afternoon and there it stayed for the next two weeks. Their car was much like Madge's but, except for a good double bed and chest of drawers, everything was company supplied;

the caboose chairs, a square table covered with heavy brown linoleum, the same as that on the floors.

As the four of us got better acquainted I began to feel sorry for Jack. He was so serious about working for the railroad, planning how he would work up to general track foreman and eventually roadmaster. What if it did take years? You needed years to learn all there was to know about track alone. He was a slim likable kid, black hair and very dark eyes. He was proud of Bev and I could see how she'd used that pride to get the diamond ring and nylons.

I tried to encourage her, but even when I took her up to Emma's she talked mostly about her home on the ranch and how it was much better than any railroad house. So I was not surprised when Jack came to our car one day after work and said she was gone. He was the saddest man I have ever seen.

"Did she say anything to you, Kay? She left a note saying I could find her at the ranch."

"You poor guy," I sympathized. "No, she didn't say a word to me."

"Bev just ain't cut out for this." He waved his hand to include the outfits, the trains, the inevitable years.

"Couldn't you find her a house somewhere?" I suggested. "And you stay here and batch through the week?"

"Her folks wouldn't go for that. Her old man wants to help me start a ranch, with horses and stuff. That's what Bev wants. I guess I'll have to."

About ten days later Bill said Jack had quit the railroad for sure, and was starting a ranch. He didn't say how he felt about it, but that night he slept with his arms tightly wrapped around me. Dear husband, I thought, I may not make it in this old baggage car — but I won't retreat. I won't be a Beverly.

During those six weeks Thatch had been developing a small but promising halo. He wasn't perfect; he still had to be coaxed and finally threatened before Bill could get him up in the mornings, and he still smoked cigarettes before breakfast until I gave up hope of ever enjoying the aroma of fresh coffee again. He did whistle when coming home late at night. Listening for his warning was better than squeaks from the cot. And he did keep his corner of the living room neat and clean, as well as his clothes.

He spent quite a few evenings in town, riding up if we happened to be going, but always walking back alone. I knew he didn't have much money to spend because he sent part of each paycheck to his mother.

It was a Wednesday evening. We were at Roy and Emma's for dinner. Roy said quite innocently, "Say, I hear your helper got in a little trouble over the week-end."

"You mean Thatch?" I asked. "Bill you didn't mention it to me."

"Well no, I didn't." My husband looked uncomfortable. "It happened over at the signal gang outfit. Nothing important."

The signal repair gang, consisting of a foreman and several young fellows, had moved into the track next to us about a week before. They had several bunkcars, and a diner with a cook. Thatch had been going over there evenings.

"Of course it's important," I told him. "I want to know about it."

Roy grinned. "You mean you don't tell your wife these things? Well Kay, it seems the boys didn't like to walk clear uptown so they invited a couple of girls down to the outfits; the kind you hire, if you know what I mean."

"Bill, is that true? And Thatch was there?"

My husband nodded. "I wasn't going to tell you, but I guess they had quite a party. Thatch stayed all night. Anyway, Sunday night they were having a repeat performance when the foreman walked in on them."

"You might say," Roy laughed, "they got caught with their pants down."

"Oh! Sometimes I think men are the most disgusting things ever invented." I looked at Emma. She was blushing but smiling at my consternation.

"I don't know," Bill put in. "In this case I'd say it was the girls."

"You would."

We drove home in one-sided silence. So that was why Thatch had spent the last two evenings in the boring sanctum of the 713. "For gosh sake, Kay, you don't have to take it so seriously," Bill argued.

I didn't reply until we'd passed a dozen yellow lamp-lighted outfits and turned in at the end of the shadowy corrals. There was a light in the 713 too. "He must be bored to death in there all alone," I said sarcastically. "I don't know if I want to sleep in that baggage car tonight."

"We have a license." Bill waited for my laugh but didn't hear any.

When we walked in Thatch was stretched out on his cot reading a magazine and listening to a brand new portable radio. Grinning sheepishly at our surprise, he said, "Battery set. Shore figured we need one."

"It sounds wonderful, Thatch!" I was so thrilled to hear a radio again I forgot that I was mad at him.

"Yeah, purty good. Play it all you want, Kay. Batteries don't cost much." He lay there on his cot with his halo, dent and all, shining in the lamplight.

So Thatch Kelly, star boarder and all man, brought my life partially back to normal. The very next morning I was back on the list of WONDER SOAP listeners. John and Sally it seemed were still not married. The sun still came out every few days, Dora still got drunk, and Thatch? Well, sometimes I could see his angelic crown and sometimes I couldn't.

Like this evening, when he was looking at the bawling cattle out there and said, "Shore reminds me of home." I'd been listening to them all day and they reminded me of a lot of things, but not of home.

But I thought there weren't quite as many cows tonight, or were we getting accustomed to them? The smell didn't seem quite as strong; of course the wind may have veered slightly. To escape the critters Bill and I agreed on a movie without knowing what the picture was. It would be a western. As the hero rode herd on a surging mass of nervous longhorns who were about to be stampeded by the villains, I could even smell the scene.

Or was it actually me?

Coming back to the outfit we were again impressed by the romantic western atmosphere around, under, and inside the 713. It was a lingering aroma; it even lingered through our love scene later. What a great chance to imagine you were in a movie! Next morning's breakfast was just like camping out on a buffalo crowded prairie.

But I'd been right. After the boys were gone to work a switch engine showed up with only ten cattle cars, which they managed to load in a mere two hours. Then, just before THE TRAVELING LIGHT program a brakeman knocked on my door.

"Got orders to move these outfits," he announced.

"You must be mistaken. My husband didn't say we were moving."

He brandished a paper. "Right here on the switch list. Outfits 713 and 787 move to Shop Track One."

In the dim past I remembered Mr. Hennesy's promise.

"Are we going, lady, or aren't we?"

It might be my only chance. I'd be right uptown where I could walk to Emma's or the store . . . electric lights . . . no cattle smells . . . no Dora . . . I said to the brakeman, "Could you help me get the steps in? I didn't know we were moving."

"Ain't my work, but all right."

"Can you wait just one more minute?" I pleaded.

"Company's paying for it, lady."

They might get impatient and leave if I took too long. I rushed around putting away a few dishes, Thatch's radio on his bed, the lamp on the floor. Then with Bucky and my coffee pot I hurried down the steps.

"Okay?" he asked.

"Yes, all right." For such a short move the kettle should stay on the stove and the cupboard doors stay closed . . . I hoped.

The brakeman boosted the steps in, climbed up to pull the door shut. The engine moved ahead pushing the ten cars of cattle and jolted them against our tool car, cattle bawling from the impact. He clung to the ladder on the 787 as the cars moved away. I took Bucky to the Buick and placed him safely on the front seat. As I started the motor the train went clacking by on another track, the 713 first, followed by the 787 and ten cars of bawling cattle with the engine bringing up the rear.

"Oh Bucky, look!" I cried. "We forgot something."

There it stood like a lonely sentinel guarding the entrance to Corral Track Five . . . our dreamhouse.

11. In The Dead Of Night

"**H**ey in there!" Someone was pounding on my front door with a club.

I turned off Thatch's radio and went to the door. A young brakeman was standing on the ground wrapping on our steps with his brake stick. "Can't put these steps here," he declared. "You got a hazard. Impaired clearance. Somebody might get hurt."

"You mean I can't have steps? I have to climb in and out, for goodness sake?" I'd been on Shop Track One for three hours and was about ready to trade back. Uptown, convenient, cleaner; it should have been named Little Grand Central. Outside my back door were tracks, switches, boxcars, smoking engines and busy profane men. They'd been pulling and slamming those cars since the moment I arrived. Between times helper engines came into the yard. Their crews would park them and simply walk away, leaving them standing with smoke drifting from the stack. There was a constant clanging of bells, toots, the slam bang of couplings which ruined my radio programs but de-lighted Bucky. He'd been singing happily all afternoon.

On the other side there was only one track that led into a yard full of iron wheels and railroad car parts. In full view of me, and vice versa, was the main street of town. Deciding my front door should face town and one track was better than fifteen, I'd shoved the steps out on that side. The other set lay in the middle of the kitchen floor.

"Can't help it," the brakeman insisted. "Rules are rules."

I felt like handing him the book of rules so he could shake it in my face. I said, "Well, you'll have to move them. I can't lift the darned things."

"I can sure do that." He jerked them away from the door, dropped them on the ground and kicked them partly under the car. Then feeling a little guilty, "Now don't forget and walk out that door."

He waved a signal and a string of freight cars rolled toward him. I had an impulse to empty some dishwater in the right place but he grabbed the ladder of a passing car and rode out of reach. The cars clicked by so close I could have touched their smudged sides, then an engine drew abreast of me and stopped. The engineer was surprised to see my face six feet from his. He was elderly, gray-headed, with a two-day beard. Recovering nobly, he smiled and touched the brim of his cap.

"Just like Grand Central Station!" I called.

"We're about through. Won't bother you anymore today."

The brakeman came along, pushed some kind of handle on the front of the engine, then held up one fist with his thumb pointing at his mouth.

"What does that mean?" I called to the engineer.

"We'll go to the waterspout and then tie up for the day." He pushed a lever and his engine hissed loudly.

"Saves time, doesn't it?" I hollered.

"Saves hollering." He pulled a handle and his iron horse started backing away. He touched his cap cordially.

I went into the living room and turned the radio back on. "Well, Bucky, maybe we'll have some peace and quiet now." But there was a new knock on the door. "Hold everything. Maybe we're moving again." It was Mr. Hennesy.

"Hello," he greeted. "Thought I'd forgot, didn't you? Everything all right?"

"Well, yes, but they won't let me put my steps up."

"That's right. Impaired clearance. You can see how a man walking along here might fall over them."

"But I can't climb that iron ladder all the time."

"Put 'em on the other side. Plenty of room there."

"For goodness sake, I thought it meant both sides!"

"No, Miz Fisher. Long as anything is six feet from the nearest rail it is okay. If you have any other problem just let me know."

I was going to say our dreamhouse was rather unhandy a mile and a half away, but that might not be his department. Bill would be home eventually and in the meantime I had my red can. With faith in the future, I looked out at my relocated front yard.

Well, it had a certain regularity about it, with acres of steel rails in a unique parallel pattern and few scattered boxcars to relieve the monotony. To my left the engine shop was smoke-blackened, with feathers of steam trailing from pipes projecting from the tin roof. Stored in a kind of tunnel made of big timbers stood a huge engine-like machine, its front entirely one large hood holding a massive, formidable looking fan painted red. That must be a snowplow. Did the snow actually get deep enough to need such a monster?

I watched two helper engines come to life and clank off through the yards coupled together, like one bulldog shoving another, and laying a new smoke screen on top of the existing one. Then a long freight train lumbered into town and ground to a stop. The fireman climbed onto the high tender, swung a waterspout around and turned on a gushing stream. It took an amazingly long time to fill the huge tank. Finally it ran over in a flood. How did he keep from getting his feet wet?

In the other direction a work train was switching cars back and forth. The engine would shove one along, then stop suddenly, letting the car coast away by itself. I saw them bang into other cars.

I had just put potatoes on to boil and set the teakettle down when . . . CRASH!

A lurching grinding earthquake struck the 713 endwise, sent me reeling and my coffee pot sliding along the drainboard toward the sink. I caught the coffee pot as I staggered by and caught myself just short of bumping into the table. The potatoes and teakettle hit the floor in a steaming splash. In the living room I heard a tinkling crash.

"Bucky! Oh . . ." He was all right, though his cage was swaying wildly. On the floor lay our radio, not Thatch's, thank goodness. I ran to the door, a different brakeman was on the ground. "What's going on here?" I demanded. "You almost knocked me down. What's the big idea?"

He glared at me. "Where's your blue flag, lady?"

"I don't know what you're talking about but you nearly . . ."

My faithful Mr. Hennesy came bustling along. "What's wrong here?"

The brakeman shrugged. "Ah, we dropped a cut down against this outfit. How'd I know it was occupied. No blue flag."

"Chris' sake, ya could see they had steps out. You might expect somebody was in 'em. You all right, Miz Fisher?"

"Yes . . . I guess so."

He said to the brakeman, "Put those steps back up for her, and next time use the brains God gave ya." It was surprising to see Mr. Hennesy angry. After the brakeman strode off he said, "He's right. No blue flag. You have one in your outfit?"

"I really don't know."

"I'll get you one." He hurried off to the car shop and in a few minutes was back with a blue-painted piece of tin shaped like a flag on an iron rod. He stuck it in the coupling on the end of our car. It was lettered MEN AT WORK.

So that was a 'blue flag'; with it dangling on our coupling I was safe, without it I was at the mercy of any and all switch engines. It didn't make sense, but that was nothing new on this man's railroad. As I gathered up the potatoes and teakettle I said in a clear determined voice, "Damn the s.b. railroads!" It made me feel a lot better. Not that I objected to being mauled by a loose freight car.

I was just getting fed up with learning everything the hard way.

The potatoes hadn't come to a boil the second time when a familiar tread stomped up the steps. It was my dear Indian chief who liked baggage cars.

"You're early," I said.

"Yeah, and good thing. I see you moved."

"And I'm ready to move back, or move out!" I told him about the crash.

"The damn fools."

"Bill, if this is living in an outfit car . . . I don't think I can take it . . . being shoved around like cattle . . . knocked off your feet . . ." I began crying.

He took me in his arms. "I don't blame you. Things like this will happen until we get wise. I should have told you about the blue flag thing but I had no idea Hennesy would move us without notice."

"Why didn't somebody else put that piece of blue tin out there if it's so important? That crew who brought us here knew I was alone in the car."

"Kay-Kay, on the railroad nobody in one department gives a damn about anybody in another department."

That seemed to be the answer to everything. If you lived in an outfit car nobody gave a damn but you. "What about the dreamhouse?" I asked.

"We'll get it first thing in the morning, before somebody steals it."

"Steals it? That thing?"

"Oh yeah, even if you don't think so it is a pretty good dreamhouse. The door fits and we got that paper dispenser. Wouldn't be surprised if somebody hasn't traded with us already." That would be the height of character, waiting for a chance to swipe an unguarded privy, but my husband was serious. "No time tonight. Can't set it up around here anyway." He said Roy told him about an outside lavatory connected to the car shop. "We get a key from the shop foreman so we can use it at night." Very generous of the foreman!

Bill examined the smashed radio and pronounced it a total loss. Then he went off to see about the lavatory key. While he was gone the electric lights came on. I stood there staring at man-made sunlight flooding my kitchen. Praise the modern conveniences. Then I thought of my shiny new refrigerator and plugged it in; it began running. Thatch came in and admired the brightly lighted kitchen; apparently he'd connected the wires. I showed him the humming refrigerator.

"Hey, how about that," he agreed.

Next morning the boys hooked a small flat trailer behind the motorcar and in a short time came putt-putting up through the yards with our functional chic-sale perched immodestly upon it. A passenger train was just pulling in but they puttered right past it as if hauling around outdoor privies was an everyday occurrence. When they came backing alongside our tool car I called, "You should have stuck a blue flag on it!"

If there were any other advantages to living in Truckee, I didn't get to experience them. Three days after moving to Little Grand Central Bill said the rail-laying program was finished. "We're moving out to Troy. Got an urgent cable job there."

"Oh dear, Madge said Troy was a miserable place."

"Sort of isolated," Bill admitted. "Probably snow there already. The boss said we have four miles of cable to repair. Might take until Christmas. I guess they were going to renew it but couldn't get new cable account of copper being scarce."

We had planned to drive to the city Wednesday night and spend Thanksgiving with my aunt and the family. So now the plan was that the outfit would move Thursday while we were gone, and we'd come back to them at Troy. The boys would have Wednesday to get things ready and do a few small jobs for Roy. I was so happy about getting away from the railroad for a day, I started putting things in the suitcase that evening.

Bill said, "What's the hurry? You got all day tomorrow."

"Never mind. I just don't want to rush and forget something." Call it premonition, or luck; before morning the suitcase and I were in for a new experience.

As sort of forewarning, the shop foreman came to the door about nine o'clock and said he had some 'bad order' cars to put on this track. Would it be all right if they put us on Track Two for the night? "Yeah, sure," Bill agreed, leaning out the door. He and Thatch pulled in the steps, disconnected the wires and took down the blue flag. "Guess we can use lamps for one evening. Almost bedtime anyway." Since it was only one switching move we'd stay in the outfit.

It was an odd sensation to have your home suddenly jolt into motion and go clicking slowly along the track while you were sitting calmly on the sofa. The lamps flickered and Bucky anxiously flew around in his cage but the old baggage car rode quite smoothly, although it creaked and groaned. In a few minutes it stopped again. "Probably shove us back in the morning. I'll just leave the steps in," Bill decided.

We were sleeping peacefully. I suppose I was dreaming of eating turkey at Aunty's and telling them about our railroad home, and how it could go moving off unexpectedly. It seemed so real, I thought I could feel an engine coupling onto the 713.

"Bill, they are moving us again."

He raised up in bed. A few lights moved past outside as we clicked over the switches. "Guess they're putting us back on Track One," he growled. "Should have put that blue flag out again." We stopped, backed up a while, went forward again. Then all was quiet and Bill's breathing came steady and undisturbed; it was amazing how this life didn't bother him. Our bedroom was bright from the gleam of lights outside. Then came the hiss of air in the brake system and Bill jumped to sitting position.

"Something's screwy," he cried. "Those are the station lights out there. We're on the main line!" In one leap he was into his slippers, pointed the flashlight at the clock and bolted from the room. I heard him jerk the door open. "What in hell's going on?"

A voice said, "You're moving to Troy, brother."

"Now?" Bill exclaimed. "This outfit doesn't move until tomorrow morning, Thanksgiving Day."

An argument blossomed and it soon sounded as if we were losing. I got up and went to see what it was all about. Thatch was leaning on one elbow, Bill was in the doorway in his pajamas confronting two brakemen outside holding their lighted lanterns.

"Look, you guys," Bill demanded, "where is your conductor?"

"He's a-comin' right now." A tall figure with an electric lantern came striding toward us from the station.

"What's the matter? I'm conductor here." It was Mr. Slate.

Bill said, "I thought Sailor Reagan had the local."

"Reagan is off sick. What's holding us up? We ain't got much time on Eighty-seven."

"How come you are moving us this morning?" Bill wanted to know. "Have you got orders to that effect?"

"Damn right I have." He held his light on a sheaf of yellow papers. "Local

94

Freight move signal outfits 713 and 787 Truckee to Troy on westward trip tomorrow, Assistant Signal Supervisor."

"He meant Thursday," Bill countered.

"We don't go west on Thursday, we go west Wednesday. You know that."

Bill stared at me. "The boss got mixed up because Thursday is a holiday. So did I. Looks like we're moving now if we like it or not." He said to Slate, "How much snow is at Troy?"

"Foot or so. What's that got to do with it?"

"We're going to the city tonight and my wife is not walking out of Troy in a foot of snow. Just wait a minute."

"Can't do it. I'm on short time for Eighty-seven."

Bill ignored him. "Kay, do you think you could leave right now? You can take your time driving to Sacramento, have the day to do a little shopping."

"For goodness sake," I stammered. "I guess so. What time is it?"

"Four AM. If you stay with the outfit we'll have to come back from Troy on a train or someway, to get the Buick. Might never get started. This way I can come in on a freight or helper and take a bus to your Aunt's. The Buick is right there behind the station."

"Well . . ."

Conductor Slate bellowed, "Listen Buster, we're pulling out in two minutes. Make up your mind."

I rushed into the bedroom, grabbed the suitcase, some underthings and shoes. Bill got my coat and purse, made sure I had money and keys. I had a feeling I was learning something the hard way but didn't know just what it was. My husband handed the suitcase and coat to a brakeman and the two helped me climb down the ladder with a bundle of pink apparel clutched under one arm. A slipper fell off and the brakeman kindly found it for me while Conductor Slate stood glowering.

Bill said, "Here, you'll have to take this damn canary. He'll freeze with all of us gone Thursday." He handed the hooded cage out to the men.

"Oh, Bill," I called from the ground, "put my pot in a safe place." Slate and the two men looked at me. I glared back. "Yes, I said pot."

Whatever they thought, it didn't delay them. Slate swung a light over his head and the cars quickly began to move. They grabbed the caboose as it came along and the stubby train went chop, chop, chop off into the night. I stood in my robe beside the track, watching the flickering red lights disappear. Then I made a clear resonant statement, out loud.

"Damn the s.b. railroads!"

I said it a couple of times while I carried Bucky across the greasy tracks and placed him on a baggage truck, then went back for the suitcase. I managed to step in a puddle of black molasses oil so my slipper stuck to the pavement at each step. With suitcase swinging, robe flying and slipper sticking, I headed for the restroom in the station, ducking low as I passed the agent's window.

In the safety of the dingy restroom I surveyed the damage. My hands were black from the iron ladder, my robe had a large greasy smudge, the slipper was a gooey mess. In the mirror I looked like a degraded version of Dora Terroli. Railroads ... husbands ... outfit cars! I slammed the sticky black slipper into the wastebasket.

"Damn the s.b. s.b. railroads."

I got into panties and bra, shoes and stockings. Wouldn't it be something if I'd forgotten a dress. I hurriedly grabbed the brown one and my hair caught in the zipper.

"Damn husbands, too," I declared, just as the toilet flushed in the stall. A motherly woman excitedly came out, stared at my suitcase, my dress half on.

"Well, I never ..." she cried. "I suppose they put you off a train, and I don't blame them!" She hurried out – to report me to the agent, no doubt.

Maybe she would. No use taking chances. I threw my robe into the suitcase and got out of there, just in time to meet the sleepy agent coming in the waiting room door.

"Lady, did you notice anybody in there acting funny?"

"Why yes," I told him. "A nice old lady without any shoes on." I turned the corner of the station, found the Buick in the dim parking area. I'd started the motor and backed part way out when I remembered poor Bucky. Like an accomplished bank robber, I left the motor running, sneaked around the building, grabbed my prize off the baggage truck and was gone in the night.

An all-night restaurant seemed a good place to wash my face and finish combing my hair. With a hundred miles of driving ahead, I decided I may as well have breakfast.

"Been driving all night?" the waitress asked.

I was tempted – just tempted, mind you – to answer, "No, I just got up from my baggage car. They're taking my husband for a ride. I've got my canary with me, though."

12. I Get Away From It All

My husband halted in the steep snowy trail ahead of me like some character out of a Jack London novel, the sack of groceries on his shoulder grotesque in the moonlight. In the whole eerie scene, only the suitcase in his hand looked modern and out of place.

Two short hours ago we'd said goodbye to my aunt and the children, and walked out of a warm house that had rugs on the floor and a tile bathroom. We'd driven through city streets with lights, people and streetcars, the memory of a happy Thanksgiving dinner still with us. We'd had that stuffed feeling from the 'little lunch' my aunt fixed, "before you start home".

Before we started home!

Somewhere behind us the Buick was parked at the edge of the woods because from there on the road was snowed in. We'd started — not walking — climbing up a meandering snowy trail in the dark. Above us the moon and a thousand stars threw long shadows across the trail. I set Bucky's cage down in the snow and asked, "You sure this isn't White Horse Pass on the trail to the Yukon?

My husband didn't answer. His breath was a thin cloud in the dim light. "How much farther?" I persisted.

"Twenty minutes. Can you make it?" He picked up the suitcase.

Our voices rang in the silvery cold silence. There was no other sound but I

Snowsheds covering westbound mainline. Ice-covered Donner Lake in the background.
(From a postcard)

felt wild eyes behind every tree. Up ahead the mountain rose toward the stars. It could have been White Horse Pass. I wouldn't have been surprised.

Bill's footsteps crunched on. I picked up Bucky and followed, taking five steps and slipping back three, my heart banging against my ribs. Somewhere far off a wild creature gave a wild barking howl. I knew what it was but didn't want to admit it. Then I slipped and dropped the birdcage. "Bucky, I'm sorry." I could hear him fluttering around inside.

My husband halted impatiently. "You and that canary. If he lives through this I'll be surprised."

I sat there in the snow looking at him silhouetted against the dim sky. "If he doesn't live it will be my warning to get out of here. You know how they use canaries in coal mines to tell if it is safe . . ."

"They don't anymore."

"When were you in a coal mine lately?"

He started on without me.

You might think twenty minutes is a short time, like twenty minutes from downtown. Well, try hiking up a vertical mountainside in the snow in the dead of night with a thousand fir trees breathing down your neck and your heart banging. If you still think twenty minutes is a short time, you will make a likely challenger of White Horse.

But the boots helped. I'd bought them the day before Thanksgiving because I wanted something for snow, just in case there actually was some. I didn't like laced ones and by the time Bill learned I'd bought cowboy boots it was too late for him to protest.

"Well, we're here," Bill announced in the dark silence.

"Just where are we?" I panted. Against the black forest was something resembling a house. A dog started barking but refused to show himself. This was coyote country all right; he knew better than to come out in anything but broad daylight. We went on, circling the house, following one of countless little trails in the snow. Judging from the tracks, an awful lot of people must live in that one house, I thought. Suddenly, amazingly we were on some railroad tracks, but the rails gleaming in the moonlight went only a hundred feet or so and disappeared into a tunnel. Fearless Fisher, shifting his pack, marched straight ahead into the awesome cavern.

"Do we have to go through there?"

"Snowsheds. Good walking now." His voice echoed with a booming sound. He swung his flashlight around and I knew what the underpinnings of the Empire State Building must be like. There were rows of great timbers standing on end, holding up a vaulted shadowy ceiling. The outside was stoutly boarded up to resemble an immense tunnel. It was a wonderful place for a person afflicted with claustrophobia. "See, plenty of room," Bill said cheerfully. "There's the other track over there." Sure, plenty of room, unless you consider the size of a locomotive.

"How much farther?" I asked. "*How much farther?*" the cavern echoed.

"Just a couple of minutes." "*Just a couple of minutes.*"

We stumbled on. There were shiny drops of oil frozen into sticky little puddles that reminded me of a good pair of slippers I'd had once, and ice, shadows, and weird sounds. We turned between the posts, crossed more dark tracks in what surely was a gargantuan mine, came to a door-like opening in the black timbered wall, and suddenly were in moonlight again.

There stood a ghostly shape — the 713. Behind it rose a towering silent mountain.

"Won't be bad if it doesn't snow anymore," the guide announced. He laid down his pack and climbed the steps with the suitcase. The glass in the door rattled as he shoved it open, then a match flared and a lamp flickered a dim welcome. He called down, "Watch that last step, it's a high one."

I stood at the top of the steps looking at the cold gloomy kitchen, snow tracks on the floor, then back outside at the huge wall of snowshed looming over us like a forbidding cliff.

"What a place to get away from it all!" I exclaimed. My breath formed a cloud in the room, my feet were frozen. "Bill, I've got to get these boots off. Could you find my new slippers in the suitcase?"

He threw the suitcase on the kitchen table and rummaged through it until everything was well scattered.

"I . . . guess you'll have to help me get the boots off," I added.

The snowsheds were cold and forbidding, like a tunnel.

He tried an experimental tug, nearly pulling me off the chair. "What did you do, get them too small?"

"They have to be tight enough to stay on! Turn around and let me put one foot against your seat." That worked.

"How will you get 'em off when I'm not around? Guess I'll have to make a bootjack." He made it sound as if building a two-car garage would be easier. "Man, it's cold in here. Good thing I drained the tanks." He went out and brought in the grocery pack, then lighted another lamp in the living room and began shaking down the ashes in the heater, the fine white cloud rising in the yellow light. "We can get lights here. Thatch and I didn't have time Wednesday. Took us most of the day just getting back to Truckee for the motorcar."

I'd forgotten the weird experience leaving Truckee; it seemed so long ago but it was only yesterday. I had to get busy to forget the cold, so I started on the load of groceries. Bill changed to overalls before he filled the tanks. This amounted to several trips in and out through the snow, rummaging in the tool car for a blowtorch, pouring more coal in the heater between times. The living room began to get warm but the kitchen and bedroom still would have frightened a penguin.

"Hey, what's that?" my husband asked on one trip. He saw the wax-paper package I was unwrapping.

"Roast turkey. Aunty gave us some to take home."

"That's right, it's Thanksgiving, isn't it."

Like me, he found it hard to believe.

With more than a month and a half since we'd left Cisco, I'd forgotten how terrible those rushing trains could be when the main track was only a dozen feet from our bedroom. Now we were back alongside the 'high iron', but with a new sound effect. The first freight train sounded like someone beating on the other end of a long sewer pipe, a hollow rumbling which steadily increased as an unseen giant stomped toward us hammering the inside of the pipe. As it went by, the outfit shook, the curtains swayed, the glass in the door rattled madly and then the countless boxcars came following one by one, clack-clack, clack-clack, clack-clack. It was Cisco all over again, only worse.

My first impression of the snowsheds had been a smothered, confined feeling and after we went to bed that black wall outside our window in the moonlight continued to bother me. Probably the knowledge of a lonely wild mountain just as close on the opposite side depressed me too. The result was no sleep.

I heard No. 28 go by about eleven, later First and Second 88 blasted through the night a half hour apart, then a freight train and another going down. Two passenger trains also went by going down. Sometime near morning one stopped in the sheds and started up again; that would be No. 210. I heard Thatch come in, stomp the snow off his shoes, and go to bed. I'd been re-living the past twenty-four hours: Waking up at four in the morning Wednesday, virtually jumping out of the outfit in night clothes, driving through the mountains for what seemed endless miles until daylight finally shone, wondering

The Dreamhouse and its tribulation trail!

about Bill riding in this crazy baggage car to some god-forsaken place called Troy. And now I knew it was god-forsaken. We were some twenty miles west of Truckee and about five miles west of the summit. Somewhere further west was Cisco and below it Emigrant Gap, where Madge was. Supposedly that was the beginning of the foothill country where there were towns and where we were supposed to work in the 'wintertime'. Still further — much further — was the city, civilization, my aunt's. It seemed impossible that a few short hours ago we were sitting around a big Thanksgiving table, laughing with the children, telling them about living in a railroad car in the mountains. They'd been awestruck, and even my aunt was a little thrilled underneath her concern. But oh! we'd put on our rose-colored glasses when we talked about it all.

Now I lay listening to the soundless night, feeling the black sheds towering over us and the wild snowy mountain at our backs, and I wondered who had a screw loose? Bill . . . or me? A baggage car with domed ceiling and cold floors . . . another man beyond the thin partition . . . snow . . .

It was the initial shock again And it was a humdinger.

Daylight came half-heartedly. In fact Bill got up and banged around getting fires started, argued with Thatch and got breakfast going by lamplight before I would believe it was morning. When I finally dragged myself to the kitchen and peered out the front door I saw why. The snowshed stood like a black wall scarcely ten feet from the outfit and was higher, dirtier and more depressing than the night before.

I looked out the back door. The dreamhouse, standing in the snow about twelve feet away, tipped its cocked roof at me. Directly behind it loomed a fir tree on a section of world jutting toward the sky, and behind that tree hung four hundred and forty-seven thousand more fir trees, all staring at me in cold maddening silence.

"Shut the door," Bill said. "You'll catch cold."

That was a practical suggestion, but in the instant before my view of the arctic was cut off I leaned out and looked straight up — I could see sky! It was obvious why daylight had arrived half-heartedly; the sun hadn't found this hole in the hills since last Fourth of July.

I had intended to visit the dreamhouse, but not now. In slippers and robe I'd have caught four kinds of pneumonia so there had to be some alternative. Thatch came into the kitchen sleepily, his hair touseled and eyes half open. I knew he'd stand beside the kitchen stove for the next five minutes dragging on a cigarette. I strode through the living room like a person hastened by nature. My hand reached out and snapped Thatch's radio full on. It blared forth, Bill hollered from the kitchen, then he stomped in to tune it down but my red can had served its purpose well muffled. I may have gloated a little in a demented way.

Troy. A forgotten hole in a forgotten section of creation.

My geranium was the first casualty. When I remembered to look at it the first morning the stalk was hanging down on the floor like a wet dishrag. I was so disheartened I just left it lying there in the corner.

Bucky was next. The poor thing lingered for days, and if the sun had come out he might have survived, but in that cold grim place he felt no incentive to fight back. He was buried with full honors out beside the dreamhouse like a fallen comrade on a polar ice trek.

Bill, realizing that I might get stir-crazy in such a place, suggested I get acquainted with the section foreman's wife. "It's not far," he assured me. "You know that house we passed coming in. He seems like a good fellow. Their name is Smith."

"Can I get there without going through the sheds?"

"Don't let those sheds worry you. We work in them all the time. You can follow the siding all but a couple of hundred feet."

"If you go with me the first time."

He considered. "Okay, we'll come in for lunch and I'll take you there."

The sun came out during the morning and though it never reached the outfit, it did start snow melting on the shed roof. The result was worse than rain; a steady downpour of big black drops. It was only about a block, but walking along the greasy tracks in that dark dripping tunnel it seemed like a mile. Reaching the end of the sheds was like finding the world again. I took a deep breath.

The section house, another hundred yards farther, stood below the track; railroad color, railroad shape, a little flat spot in front that probably was a meager lawn in summer. It stood against a dark green forest that fell away like a toboggan slide.

"You can make it from here," Bill said, "so I'll take off."

"If I'm not home you'll know I was afraid to go back through the sheds."

A path led from the track down to the house, and dozens of other little trails ran in all directions around the house and off into the woods. The front porch was cluttered with parts of a child's wagon, several shovels and a pair of snowshoes, the first I'd ever seen. I could hear a radio playing.

When I knocked on the loose screen door someone came to a window and peeked. Something smelled like spring, but nothing around this lonely home looked like spring. After several minutes the door was opened by a frail woman with a pleasant face.

"For golly sake!" she exclaimed. "The children said there was a lady at the door but I didn't believe them." She had a towel wrapped around her head and a paint brush in her hand. The odor of fresh paint met me.

"I'm Kay Fisher, from the signal outfit. I thought I'd come get acquainted."

"Golly sake come in, Mrs. Fisher." She held the screen door open and it stayed that way. "Why, I'm near speechless to think anybody come to visit me."

I said, "Are you painting at this time of year?"

"I do it to pass the time." She had blue eyes, light colorless hair and protruding teeth; she couldn't have weighed much over a hundred pounds. The living room was like Emma's with high old-fashioned ceilings, narrow windows. There was a leather davenport and leather chair, cheap floor lamp and worn carpet on the floor. She told me, "I painted all these downstairs rooms last winter. Helps keep me busy."

I wondered why the walls were so dark now. The ivory color looked as if it had been there for years.

"You come on right in the kitchen and we'll have some coffee. The children are having lunch . . ." She led the way through a short dark hall which didn't seem to have any purpose except a steep stairway leading up from it . . . "or I thought they were!"

The kitchen was more old-fashioned with a huge iron stove, numerous unhandy cupboards and a large table covered with white oilcloth. One little girl with stringy blonde hair was eating, her short legs dangling from a much painted kitchen chair.

"Please don't bother, Mrs. Smith. Go right on with your painting."

"Golly no. Please call me Millie. I got all winter to finish the paintin'."

She put the paint brush on a newspaper on the drainboard and fussed with a large battered percolator. The little girl stared at me and ate her bread at the same time. Millie said, "Kay, take one of those chairs by the table. Why the children didn't finish. Summie, where did they go?"

"They're hidin',"

"Hiding? Where?"

"In the B R. They're scared."

"Well, golly sake." Millie went to a door opening off the kitchen and immediately there was a stampede of scurrying feet toward other parts of the house. "I don't know what's come over them. Why, I guess they're just bashful." She poured coffee into heavy mugs and handed me one on a saucer. The table held a plate full of sliced homemade bread, several jars of jam, heavy glass tumblers filled with knives, forks and spoons. On the wall were numerous coats and sweaters on nails.

I said to the little girl, "What's your name?"

"Dolores."

"Oh, that's a nice name."

Millie explained, "We call her Summie for summer. Their father gives them all nicknames."

"But my name is Dolores."

"Well, that's what I'll call you then," I told her. She smiled shyly and ran out of the room.

"Summie, you tell the others to come finish eating," Millie called. There was a flurry of tittering in the hall. "Oh, there they are. Now all of you quit acting up. Come now."

They came, all five of them. All blonde, bashful, all casting sidelong glances at me, with much scraping of chairs and fighting over the jam jars.

"Now that's better," Mrs. Smith admonished. "Children, this is Mrs. Fisher. She lives in a outfit car and she's come to see us. Kay, this is Tinky, he's ten. We call him that because he's always a-tinkerin', but his name is Thomas. And this is Mary, she's eight. We call her Boatsie."

"Eight and a half." Boatsie put in.

None would look up as she introduced them but if I looked away, all eyes were on me. There was another boy about six, Richard but called Rip. Summie was four and the smallest boy, John, was three. He was Jo-Jo.

"My, you certainly have a nice family," I assured her, "but why the nicknames?"

"Their father sorta names them, he says according to how they turn out." The children ate without speaking and then all disappeared but Summie. She sat and watched me.

"How long have you lived here, Millie?"

"My, we been here I guess six years," she replied. "Maybe we'll get out this comin' summer. Golly, I hope so. I'm gettin' tired up of snow."

"Does it get deeper later on?"

"The snow? Oh yes, we had twelve feet two year ago."

"Twelve feet of snow?" I could hardly imagine her pinned up in this house miles from anywhere with five children and twelve feet of snow. "What do you do?" I worried. "How do you get groceries?"

"We have stuff shipped on the local." She poured more coffee. I looked at the old kitchen and all the evidences of daily life in this little self-sufficient family, and thought, what have I to complain about? She went on, "I do a lot of sewin', and a'course," she laughed, "paintin'. Summie and Jo-Jo are too small to ski yet but the others do. They're pretty good at skiin'."

"I'm goin' to this year!" Summie declared.

"A'course you are," Mrs. Smith agreed. "Kay, would you like to see my paintin'?"

She was pleased when I said yes. We climbed a narrow stairway to three small bedrooms with sloped ceilings. She had crowded the children into two rooms and was painting the front one a light green to cover a dingy, smoke-stained cream color. A small radio on a stool was playing away.

"Millie, it really looks nice," I told her.

"Golly, you can see the rooms get awful dirty. Seems like the wind brings the train smoke right inside."

It became an amazing afternoon. Millie gladly abandoned her work to relate where and when each of the children were born, of the various winters, of her hopes. Her main interest was the children and from them she drew the fortitude to live in such a place.

They had an automobile in a shed behind the house but it was of little use in winter. When I said ours was parked down near the highway she was immediately interested. "Tain't far to Cisco," she suggested. "We might walk down to your car and go there someday. The children can come along and help carry stuff."

"But what about the little ones?"

She explained that Boatsie would stay with Summie and Jo-Jo. When she said 'children' she meant whomever among them was concerned. But it was always 'the children', never 'the kids'.

To me, the idea of walking down that mountain to the car sounded preposterous but little Summie, who had been following us around, suddenly disappeared. In a minute all of the children came into the kitchen wide-eyed. Tinky whispered in his mother's ear.

"Oh Tinky, not today." She smiled at me. "They want to know if we're goin' to Cisco today."

Their sudden disappointment was pathetic but it did have the effect of breaking down their bashfulness. They stayed listening to our talk, and when I asked them, told me about skiing. I said I was afraid of the snowsheds so Tinky promptly volunteered to walk back with me.

"Is it all right?" I asked Millie.

"Golly yes. They're used to the sheds. They can all go exceptin' Jo-Jo acourse." That brought a loud reaction from Jo-Jo, who began to cry. The rest ran for their coats and overshoes. I hadn't thought of going just then but it seemed my escort was chomping at the bit.

Millie Smith and Tinky, Boatsie, Rip, Summie and Jo-Jo became my saviours at Troy. They made me feel I should count my blessings — even if I had to look carefully to find some.

The children were thrilled with my outfit car and came every day no matter what the weather. I often walked back with them to visit Millie. They would listen like little rabbits to see if a train was coming before we started through the sheds. We made one trip to Cisco, taking along a toboggan sled to haul the groceries back up the hill. Going down, the three children who'd come along jumped on the sled and went careening down the winding trail. Of course they piled up at each turn but that only made it more exciting.

When we parked the Buick again and loaded everything onto the sled it amounted to quite a load. I'd found that I'd better have enough supplies for two weeks or more, and Millie had stocked up on fresh milk and vegetables, even though the prices were high. As we began climbing, with all helping to pull the sled, I was reminded by panting breath and aching legs what an isolated place this was. Millie kidded me about having to stop and get my wind. Evidently you had to be born in these mountains to survive.

I learned something else from this shy woman with a simple name and five children — how to make sourdough batter. At first the idea sounded rather unpleasant but she assured me it was a life-saver.

"I'll give you a starter," she insisted one day. She ladled a pint of white creamy batter from a large bowl into a smaller one, which she covered with wax paper. "Golly, it makes the best hotcakes. And biscuits! I don't know what I'd do without it."

I looked at the white mass, which smelled like stale beer. "Well, how do you use it?"

I was hardly enthusiastic, but breakfast with us had been expensive and complicated. Bill and Thatch woke up every morning with appetites that would shame a hungry bear in spring. My few trials at hotcakes produced thin brown wafers which Bill complained "just didn't stick to your ribs". If there was a chance to make a lusty breakfast with this unlikely concoction, I would at least try.

"It's easy as pie, Kay," Millie said. "When you get home now, add in about that much agin of white flour and water. Not too thick. Just sit it away in the kitchen where it ain't too hot nor too cold. If it's too thick it won't work, and if it's too cold it won't neither."

How would I know if it were too hot, too cold, or too thick?

"Then to make a batter," she went right on, "you take about half sourdough and the rest anythin' you want. You add . . ."

"I'm lost," I interrupted. "What is anything?"

She laughed. "Any kinda flour, whole wheat or white, and acourse salt, sugar and a egg. Mix all that up and the last thing put in a teaspoonful of soda soaked in water."

"To this?" I held up the little bowl.

"Golly, no! That's your starter. Keep that all the time. Just take out some and put back some, but don't use it all." The more she talked the more confused I became. The small bowl in my hand seemed to have stupendous possibilities but, like Pandora's box, I was afraid to chance it.

After getting her to repeat the secret procedure several times, I gathered that this mixer had the effect of yeast, but it could be carried along from day to day as long as you added as much as you took away. It was just one ingredient, to be mixed into the actual batter and baking soda added at the last moment. Holding the potent mixture gingerly, I started home. Millie added one last instruction. "Now if you have any trouble makin' it work in the mornin', you come back."

I came back. The foamy sticky dish I brought with me was only part of my trouble in 'making it work'. The rest was on the floor of my kitchen and down the sides of the box on which I'd set the bowl.

Millie took one expert look at the mess. "Golly, you got it too warm."

"I was afraid it would be too cold so I put it on a box back away from the stove," I said, disheartened. I didn't tell her the outfit smelled like a brewery.

"It's got to be room temperature," she advised. "I'm makin' biscuits for supper tonight. I'll send some over with the children, and a new starter."

Room temperature in our outfit varied from a hundred degrees near the stove to thirty above in the bedroom but I decided to chance too cold rather than too hot next time. There had to be a next time; admitting defeat in face of Millie's lackadaisical success was unthinkable.

Besides, the biscuits were wonderful. My husband and his hungry assistant brightened as only a male can when sampling good food. I was lucky to get one feather-light biscuit for myself. Of course Bill wanted to know who made them and why his wife couldn't make biscuits like that, so I had to tell him about sourdough. He smelled the starter, smelled the biscuits and had me tell him the process.

"Forms an acid," he decided. "The soda reacts with it. Same principal as baking powder only better. Where did Mrs. Smith learn it?"

I didn't know, but my hopes for success rose. Next morning with my husband sticking his nose thoroughly into the ritual, we tried making hotcakes.

"The real McCoy," Bill proclaimed from the table.

Thatch agreed they were, "Not bad."

When I told Millie she acted as if she knew all along what the result would be. When I asked if her mother had given her the recipe I got a surprise.

"Golly, Charlie taught me about it. He learned it in Alaska from a prospector. He said in the goldrush when they had to pack way in, bakin' powder was no good. It wouldn't last and it was spoilt if it got damp. But sourdough worked fine. They carried the starter right in top the flour sack. Jes packed dry flour around it instead of a bowl."

"Is that why they are called Sourdoughs?" I wondered.

She looked surprised. "Why, I guess so. I never did think about it, but we can ask Charlie."

Charlie Smith was a chunky, pink-faced man who seemed to be more interested in fishing and the children than in railroading. When we visited a few times in the evening he acted as if we were old friends. He didn't say take off your coat and sit down; he expected you to do so. He was serious about world affairs, enthusiastic about fishing, and all smiles when the children were around. Summie or little Jo-Jo could bring him their troubles and nothing else mattered for the moment. Yet he didn't appear to worry about their education or training.

He'd leave his overshoes right in the way on the front porch or fishing pole standing in a corner of the kitchen, but there was always coffee and pie if we came over, and we were expected to accept it. Arguments about too much coffee late at night would not be listened to.

I'd wondered about the children's schooling. We moved there Thanksgiving week but the following Monday they were due back in school. It was then I learned that Tinky, Boatsie and Rip, who was only six, walked every day down to the highway. There they caught a bus and rode six miles, repeating the process on the way home. It meant getting up at six o'clock to hurry off down the mountain, and trudging back again as darkness was falling. If it snowed too much they simply missed a day. In December the school closed

109

for winter and opened again in April, so the poor little Smiths got their vacation in the worst part of a year and none at all in summer.

I could understand how Millie felt when she said, "Golly, I hope we get out this year."

Six years of hoping, working, painting, raising her family. Railroads were cruel. I could expect perhaps six weeks in this hole in my baggage car. I was lucky.

13. Snow!

Bill's boss said the job at Troy had to be finished no matter how long it took. But they couldn't repair cable when it was snowing, so it snowed for two, three days at a time. Several times they were forced to come in by noon, well aware that one more day had been added to the time we were doomed to stay here. I hated the place as much as they did but I knew they needed my moral support. I wondered why the work was so important.

Bill explained, "The cable carries all the circuits for the block signals. Some of it really is in bad shape, but we're over the worst part. About a mile left to go."

"And if you don't fix it?"

"The signals will quit working. Trains would be stalled."

That was reason enough. I went on frying stacks of hotcakes every morning and wracking my brain to make meals that would satisfy my two hungry boarders. We were running out of food and Bill had to phone the roadmaster to get some supplies to us on the local freight. As December began the weather seemed to pause for a new onslaught. We had a week of clear cold days. Bill got orders to work that Sunday if possible.

"Kay, why don't you walk down the track and see what we're doing?" he suggested. "We're less than a mile away now. You can bring our lunches out."

Glad to get away from the outfit for a few hours, I agreed. About noon I stopped at Millie's to see if any of the children wanted to go along. Boatsie and Rip were thrilled to be my escort, so the three of us started out. The tracks were bare of snow but on each side large smudged patches of it lay frozen solid.

"Missus Kay, you'll see a nice view pretty soon," Boatsie promised.

We tramped along single file, the children each carrying a lunch bucket. The wind made our noses cherry-red. The tracks curved through a rocky cut for half a mile, then opened out high up on the mountainside.

"Here's where the view is," they announced.

Stretching for miles below us lay a valley and a panorama of mountains under a sky crowded with billowy clouds. The dark green forest lay like a great rug across the valley, and being too large, reached up the sides of the hills. Threading through the scene was the silver twine of highway.

"It is really beautiful," I agreed.

"There's your daddy up there."

Above us on the brushy slope I saw the pole line and high in the sky, hanging on the wires like a spider was my husband, in some kind of chair on pulleys, his feet swinging in the air. He waved.

"Bill Fisher, come down!" I cried. "You'll fall."

He shook his head and hollered to Thatch standing on the ground beside a bonfire. Thatch began pulling the seat along the cable with a long rope. The seat swayed back and forth recklessly and I shuddered to think of the rocky ground below.

"Is that all you do, Thatch?" I called.

"Yep. Come on up by the fire."

The seat carrying my husband bumped against a pole and he clambered out, clutching the pole with his climbing spurs. When he reached the ground his lips were blue with cold.

"Well, I didn't know you were doing anything like this," I declared. I stared up at the tiny seat and wires stretching through space. "What if you fell out?"

He slapped his hands and held them to the fire. "Don't worry; I'm well buckled in, but my feet sure freeze up."

"Does Thatch go up some of the time?"

Thatch grinned. Bill said, "He's only assistant signalman. Not qualified to ride a cable chair."

I looked at this wild windy country with its brush, dirty snow, and curving railroad tracks. "Is it worth it?" I asked.

"Is it worth what?"

"Whatever we're working for."

*There was Bill in some kind of a chair
on pulleys, his feet swinging in the air.*

He looked up at the little seat and the wires humming in the wind. "The cable is pretty bad. Somebody's got to do it."

We sat around the fire to eat. Close to the ground we were more protected from the wind and could enjoy the scenery. I said what a shame we couldn't have the view without being so isolated.

"Pretty," Bill agreed, "but it's a rugged place to build a railroad."

"Hey, here comes Tinky," Rip told us. "He's sure hollerin'. Yea Tinky, we're up here."

Tinky came scrambling up the slope toward us. "War! War!"

"Take it easy," Bill said. "What's wrong?"

"The Japanese army is bombin' our army and we're gonna bomb them! The roadmaster called Daddy and he's getting the section crew out so we'll be ready when they come ashootin'."

"Wait a minute, Tinky. You say they called your Dad?"

"Sure, just now. We're startin' a war right away!"

"We'd better go to the house," Bill said quietly. "Might be just a scare."

It was true. The phone lines were crackling with instructions to section foremen to put men at all tunnels and bridges and watch for attempts at sabotage. The only attack had been at Pearl Harbor, more were expected.

"They're crazy," Bill declared. "They haven't got a chance."

"Done a lot of damage so far," Charlie told him. "Thirty battleships sunk at Pearl Harbor already."

"Thirty! Holy smoke."

Through the afternoon we began to get an inkling of what had happened. Wild reports came over the phone lines. By evening we could get reception on the Smith's radio. Congress had been called into emergency session and declared war on Japan. Troops were being mobilized. Trains were being searched at Truckee and Colfax, National Guard units called to patrol yards and roundhouses. Charlie was instructed to do the best he could with his few men to guard his tunnel and two bridges against fifth columnists.

As Millie began filling his lunch bucket Charlie explained that he'd stay at Lower Cascade Bridge all night, checking with his other men by trackside telephone. He got his coat and a deer rifle from the closet. "You keep listenin' on that phone, Millie. If the line goes dead sudden like . . ."

Bill said, "Don't worry, we'll stay with her."

I looked at Millie. She was biting her lip.

There was no attempted sabotage that night but the next day there was plenty of action. Troy took on the appearance of an armed camp as National Guard units began to arrive. They ground up and down the road in powerful trucks, strung temporary phone lines through the sheds and tunnels, issued passes to Bill and Thatch. We heard that the ski lodges around Norden were being taken over for barracks. Bill was instructed to have lights and identification along if he had to be out at night, and he said it was no joke. Many of the guards were young fellows, scared and trigger-happy as they patrolled with shotguns or automatic rifles slung over their shoulders. It was a shaky feeling to realize that the United States had been attacked by a foreign country.

But life in the 713 went on as unpredictably as before. A week later Thatch got off No. 210 on Monday morning with a squirming black bundle under his jacket. "Thought you might like a pup, Kay," he explained. He put the little fellow down on the kitchen floor.

"Why, Thatch, he's cute! What made you think of a dog?"

"Oh, account of your canary dying. He ain't housebroke."

He snapped his fingers and the pup wiggled over to him, leaving a trail of yellow water. When Bill came in from the tool car he was met by a shrill "yap-yap-yap."

"Where did the pooch come from?"

"I brought him for Kay."

Bill mulled over the idea. "I dunno. We really don't need a dog."

Cab-in-Front locomotive heading Second Section of the westbound Overland at Troy, Calif.

"I can't keep him," Thatch announced. "I'm leaving."

"Leaving? How come?"

"Gonna enlist in the Navy."

Perhaps it was the darkness of the kitchen, but his halo seemed to shine all of a sudden. I realized he liked us more than we knew. Living with us in the baggage car all this time, he'd trod a narrow path between our privacy and his own comfort.

Bill phoned the signal supervisor who said to let Thatch leave immediately without the required ten day notice, so he packed his tin suitcase.

"I'm leaving you the radio, too, Kay."

"Thatch! If my husband weren't right here I'd kiss you."

"Shore glad he's here."

"We'll call the dog 'Thatch'."

"Aw, I wouldn't want him to get stuck with a moniker like that. Why not call him 'Monday'?"

With that Thatcher Kelly walked out of our lives, and Monday wiggled in. He was to discover a wonderful world of constantly changing smells, and become our constant companion. He was to learn about squirrels, jackrabbits, porcupines, engines, brakemen, snowplows, and that the Buick was a Gibraltar that would not move without us, but the baggage car might go rolling off at any time. His first lesson, though, concerned my broom. If it smacked him on the tail it meant "You little so-and-so, you wet the floor again".

The next morning it was snowing so Bill wasn't enjoying his breakfast, but I had some news to help him forget the weather.

"Bill, there is water running out of the cookstove."

"Water?" He got up and came to look. "Holy smoke, the hot water coil is broken. Have to call the company plumber."

"Call the plumber! In these mountains? I suppose that means we'll get the stove working sometime next month."

"I can shut off the hot water line and get the stove working. Might have to use the teakettle for a while."

I had visions of pots and kettles on both stoves as I tried to keep up with the demand for bath water, dishes, laundry. He went tramping off to the telephone shanty. In a little while he was back, mysteriously measured the firebox with his steel tape and went off again. Next trip he shoveled the remains of the fire out into a snowbank and casually announced the plumber would be here by noon and should have the stove fixed shortly thereafter.

"I don't believe it," I told him.

"Kay, I talked to the man on the phone and he said he'd be here. There isn't any reason to think he won't."

"Well, if you can get the stove fixed on such short notice, why can't you get the tool car roof fixed? You've been reporting for months that it leaks."

"That's different."

Like everything else on the railroad. Besides, the tool car roof wasn't leaking now with two feet of snow on top of it. After he'd gone to work I swept up the water, shoveled out the rest of the muddy ashes. Then I sat down to wait for a miracle. Sure enough, a helper engine stopped about noon and a few minutes later there was a knock on the door. Monday happily went to the door thinking it was Bill, then started yapping wildly at the apparition on our steps.

"Are . . . you the plumber?"

He was a tall rangy man with bright grey eyes, but first you noticed the big overshoes with overalls crammed into the tops. Holding onto our wildly barking dog, I could not avoid staring at the dirty overalls, his mackinaw with an oily rag hanging from one pocket, the once fur-lined cap, now a floppy headpiece of uncertain color and more uncertain age.

He had needed a shave for some time and you sort of discovered that he must be sixty years old. He leaned forward from the weight of a sack of tools on his shoulder. "Sorry to track in this snow," he said. "Got a broom? I'll sweep it out."

"Never mind," I told him. I couldn't believe he was a plumber, actually here to fix my stove.

"Fine dog you got there. Fine dog." He emptied the sack of tools on the floor, then took off the stove lids and piled them in a sooty jumble in a corner.

"Fine stove. Got one just like it I've had for twenty years."

Twenty years, forty years! Wasn't anything or anybody young on this railroad? "How did you get here so soon?" I asked him.

"Came on a light engine from Norden," he replied. "Always expect a call when there's an outfit around. Nothing ever goes wrong on sunny days."

"Will you be able to fix the stove?"

"Of course I'll be able to fix it, if your husband gave me the right measurement." He whipped out a steel tape and rechecked, wiping the soot from his tape with a smudged thumb. "Good man, that Fisher. Right on the ball."

I didn't know if Bill was such a good man but I knew he was right on the ball, when it came to this pioneer living anyway. The man tossed his mackinaw on the floor, disclosing a tattered khaki shirt with sleeves cut off just below the elbow, evidently with a pocket knife, and went to work with the direction of one who knew what he was doing. He didn't lay a tool down, he dropped it, but never had to look for the correct one; they were all under his feet.

The banging went on most of the afternoon, with Monday alternately creeping in to smell things and leaping back to avoid a dropped wrench. When the floor was thoroughly tracked with soot and water and the temperature hovering around zero, he rattled the lids into place, wiped them with the oily rag and announced the job was done.

"Always try to rush a cookstove job," he observed. "Women get all excited when their stove won't work."

"Well, thanks for coming so soon. Are you married?"

"Married? I should say not!"

"That's too bad."

"Yes, I'd have made a good meal ticket for some wife." Monday, who had decided our visitor wasn't such a bad guy after all, followed him to the door. "Fine dog," the plumber said.

"What is your name?"

"Woods. They call me The Parson."

"Were you a preacher?"

"No. Thought about being one, but I couldn't see preaching to people too busy making money to listen. Same with marriage. You think a woman wants you, but you find out she just wants a fur coat."

With that profound observation Mr. 'Parson' Woods departed, leaving me wondering where common sense left off and eccentricity began in these parts. The repair job was a stroke of luck considering the weather, or so I thought, until I turned on the hot water tap. It now disgorged oil instead of water, then a mixture of the two. I also discovered that Mr. Woods had slopped over on one of his connections; as the fire got going there was a persistent dripping sound. Well, that would be good news for the worker-of-miracles, Bill Fisher.

"Hiya, wife," Bill greeted when he got home. "How about an extra for dinner?" Behind him, sack and all, was The Parson.

"Well, I'll have to talk to this gentleman first," I said pointedly. "That pipe you fixed is leaking."

He brushed past, went to the stove and peered behind it. "Can you beat that? First time I ever had a thing like that happen." He poured his tools on the floor and took off his mackinaw.

Oh, no, not again! I thought.

Presently he pronounced the faulty joint fixed for sure this time. But from then on we always knew when the water was getting too hot; The Parson's special pipe connection would start dripping.

If it sounds weird to sit down at a dinner table in an ancient baggage car with a snowy mountain outside, and a husband who is thoroughly enjoying himself; just add a third in the form of The Parson and the scene becomes preposterous. It seemed he had no way to get home, no east train until about 7 PM, so Bill insisted he should stay and eat with us.

"Fine dinner," he assured me. "Takes a woman to give it the right touch."

"Are you getting enough?" I asked.

"Now you wouldn't expect me to say no, Mrs. Fisher. A bachelor is never critical of a free meal."

"How is it you never married?" Bill put in.

"Your wife asked me the same thing." He laid down his fork to give the matter his full attention. "Long time ago I decided I didn't want a wife tagging me around. They tie a man down, they're fussy; they want clean towels and sheets, fancy dishes. They get all worked up if a man wants to go out and have a good time."

"Didn't you ever want children?" I wondered.

"Children? Why, that's just an instinct the good Lord injected into us so the population wouldn't die out. I've probably got a half dozen kids running around I don't know about."

Yes, fantastic described the dinner exactly. But The Parson was interesting when he got warmed up to his subject.

"Of course, in my younger days I had a couple of close calls," he admitted. "One waitress got pretty serious about me. She took to standing real close when she put my order on the table. One day I put my hand down and touched her leg. She had a nice shape, too. Pretty soon she moved off, past a table with a pitcher of ice water. Well, she reached in, grabbed a piece of ice and slung it at me. That woman had an arm like a Brooklyn pitcher!"

"Hit you?" Bill asked.

"Right on the noggin. See that scar?"

The Parson, I decided, was a character. He said he'd worked in the days when it 'was really tough'. He remembered the first motorcars, gasoline monstrosities built like the old handcars, that stayed on the track only by the grace of Saint Peter. "Luck and plenty of wrenches."

"Did you work through the depression?" Bill wanted to know.

"Know how I managed to keep my job? I had a big pipe wrench three feet long, carried it all the time and never wore clean overalls. I was the only man on the pike that looked busy."

I wondered if I should tell him the Depression was over and he could change his overalls now. Bill checked the time, put on his coat and slipped a red flare, called a fusee, into his pocket. The Parson thanked me for the dinner, patted the dog, and followed Bill down the steps.

"Monday dog," I laughed. "What would Aunty think if she saw us tonight?"

The weather stayed clear and cold for the next few days as Bill strove to finish the cable, using one of Charlie's men as a helper. Finally he said it was done except for a few spots that would go through the winter all right. But when he called his boss he was told to help the Cisco maintainer for a day or two installing blackout hoods on the signals.

It seemed hard to believe that enemy bombers could attack California, but after the Pearl Harbor disaster anything was possible. We'd heard on the news of air raid alerts and blackouts in the coastal cities with people appointed as block wardens to enforce the regulations. He said it was a miserable job climbing around over the signal bridges, working with small screws and cold fingers. It turned cloudy and windy again but they were able to convert all the signals from Norden to Crystal Lake sheds.

Worried about another storm catching us before we could move, he called in one morning, reported all the hoods installed, then learned a new helper had arrived but got off the train at Norden instead of Troy.

"Darn it," he fumed, "I figured on today to load up our gear and the motorcar, be ready to move out of here by tomorrow. Now I guess I'll have to go up to Norden and get him, and the weather report stays storm. Well, with a little luck we still might make it."

"If you think we might I'd like to go over to Millie's and say goodbye. They've been so nice to us."

"Okay. I should be back before noon. Better make two lunches; that guy probably won't have one."

After he'd gone I put on a warm coat for the walk to Mrs. Smith's. The

After a storm. Rotary plow with wide wings extended cutting out center core and widening righthand bank, near Spruce Station.

sky was gray and threatening. As I walked along in the sheds the wind moaned in the high timbers overhead.

"Golly, ain't it cold?" Millie said at the door. "Sure going to storm."

"What has it been doing most of the time?"

"Oh, we ain't had nothin' but flurries. But see how low the clouds is? This'll be a good'n."

Millie Smith knew her mountain weather. In an hour the wind was rattling the windows and howling around the corners of her house. It drove the leaden clouds so low they swept the treetops. Snow began like tiny white leaves driven before the wind and the forest faded beyond the curtain of white flakes. She turned on some lights, upstairs the radio sputtered unintelligibly. About noon the lights went out. The storm seemed to close in, shaking the old house and plastering the window screens with snow. Millie lighted some lamps.

"Bill should be back," I told her. "I'd better go back to the outfit."

"Golly, I'm worried about the children. When it's stormin' the school bus brings 'em early. But it's gettin' awful bad out there."

"What can you do about the children, Millie?"

"I'll phone up pretty soon and see if the bus took out."

I didn't realize how bad it was until I started to go. When I turned the knob the wind slammed the door against me. The porch was a mass of swirling snow.

"Why, it's wild out there!" I cried.

"Golly sakes, there's nearly a foot already. Kay, don't walk in the tracks. You'd never hear a train in such a wind."

I nodded and waded up the path. The tracks were obliterated in the swirling whiteness, my own footsteps were being swept away. Now I couldn't even see the house behind me. I took a few more steps, felt one of the rails under the snow, and crossed hurriedly. I tried to look into the stinging wind but my eyes smarted. Ahead, the sheds were a black outline, like a ghostly ship hidden in fog, but it gave me direction.

Head down I staggered along, snow sifting around my knees. It was weird that just a short while ago I'd walked on dry gravel, stepping over shiny rails. Now only the sheds told me that I was safely to one side of those dangerous tracks. I stopped for breath, turning my back to the wind.

Then I saw a figure in army boots and rifle over his shoulder walking in the middle of the track. He seemed to be wading in a white drifting sea.

"Don't walk there!" I called. "You might get hit."

"What?" he shouted. The wind smothered his words. Suddenly a yellow headlight plunged at us out of the storm.

"Look out!" In panic I grabbed his coat and jerked him out of the way. We both fell in a cloud of slamming snow as the locomotive thundered past and disappeared in the void.

He struggled to his feet. "Holy cow, lady. You saved my life."

"Never walk in the tracks when you can't hear," I shouted.

He nodded gratefully and swayed away into the storm.

I halted when I reached the sheds, my heart thumping. The timbered cavern was like a cave in some Siberian wilderness. Earthly things like houses and paved streets simply couldn't exist anymore. I wasn't sure that grubby baggage car even existed, but there were footprints leading up through the sheds. Bill must be home. Snow had drifted around the cars. It swirled in my face as I climbed the steps and pushed open the door.

"Bill?" The outfit was dark and cold, but someone was in the living room. Our dog was all excited. A strange kid was there, spreading blankets on Thatch's cot.

"Who are you? The new helper?" He was about nineteen with blonde hair and pockmarked adolescent skin.

"Yeah," he answered, "but I dunno if I'm going to like it here. They didn't tell me about this snow."

"They didn't tell me either."

"And I didn't expect any woman here."

"You are in for a lot of surprises. Where's Bill?"

"Ya mean Mr. Fisher? He left a while ago to fix some wires somewheres."

Bill out in that storm! I wondered if he'd eaten. The only thing to do was get the place warmed up and straighten out this kid. I looked at him standing with his mouth open.

"What's your name?" I said.

"Huh? Joe Kneebone."

"Well, Joe, stir up that fire while I go and change shoes."

"I dunno anything about them kind of stoves."

I jerked open the stove door and stirred down the ashes until the grates rang. "Well, take that bucket and get some coal from the other car. And bring some kindling." Monday followed him.

I went into the bedroom to get my wet boots off. In a few minutes I felt a cold blast of air and came out to find him dumping huge lumps into the heater. The end door of the outfit was wide open, snow pouring into the kitchen.

"Wait a minute!" I cried. "You can't start a fire with lumps like that. For goodness sake close the door. Where's Monday?"

"Huh?"

"The dog."

"I dunno."

I ran to the end door. The doorway into the tool car was wide open too, and snow drifting in. "Monday? Hey, Joe what's-your-name, come and see if you can find him." He plodded disgustedly out to the tool car. In a minute he was back.

"He ain't there."

"Well, he can't be far," I declared. "Look around outside."

His expression hinted I might have lost my marbles, but he got his cap and jacket and marched out. I lighted two of the wall lamps and then began to unload lumps of coal from the sooty belly of the heater. I dropped them one at a time on the floor.

"Damn the s.b. railroads. Damn the s.b. s.b. . . . ."

Joe Shinbone was standing in the passageway, gaping. He had a wet shivering bundle in his arms.

"Monday! You poor thing."

"He was underneath your living car."

I threw a towel around the shaking pup and put him in his box. He was whimpering pathetically, his little teeth chattering. Joe was still in the same spot, in the same position, his mouth still open. "What's the matter with you?" I scowled, looking at his pimpled face and frightened eyes. "You think I'm crazy, don't you?"

"I wasn't thinking nothin' like that."

"Don't kid me. In fact you may be right. For goodness sake you left the door open again." I strode past him into the snow-sprinkled kitchen and slammed the door. "Now look, Joe, there are some things to learn around here. The first one is always shut the door!"

"Well, I don't think I'm going to stay . . ."

"That's up to you, but for now you are stuck here."

He stood there while I threw paper, kindling and coal into the pot-bellied heater with grim enthusiasm. Probably he was worried about having blundered into a hole full of crazy people, or that I might start swearing again. Not that I cared. The main thing was to get the room warm and some canned milk heated for my poor pup. Outside, the storm was getting worse.

"Joe, did Bill say where he was going? How long he'd be gone?"

"He didn't tell me nothing."

I listened to the wind. The baggage car swayed gently from the force. Then I heard someone struggling to push the door open. "Millie!"

She was breathless and covered with snow, her lips quivering. "The children ain't come. I'm worried. Could you stay with the little ones? I'm going down to see what's happened."

"You can't walk down to the highway in this storm!"

"Golly sakes, if I can't walk down the children sure can't walk up. Charlie ain't come in. The phone is dead, I can't find out about the bus."

She had thought of everything, had even waited too long before coming to get my help. "Of course I'll come. Joe, find some of Bill's rainclothes in the tool car. You go with her."

I put Monday's milk on the floor and struggled into my wet coat and boots. As we started out I couldn't see how so frail a woman could walk at that speed. We plowed heads down across the windswept path between the sheds and her house. I marveled at her sense of direction.

"I sorta hoped Charlie would be here but he ain't. Golly, I guess you can see I better go. The children's couldn't break trail in this." She turned away into it with Joe tagging behind. I asked God to go with her.

The living room was lighted by a single lamp, on the wall the crank phone hung silent. I could hear the voices of Jo-Jo and Summie in the kitchen so I joined them and we sat at the table looking out at the blowing snow. Half an hour later I heard her husband on the porch.

"Hi," he said when I opened the door. "Some storm."

"Charlie, your wife has gone looking for the children. They haven't come home."

He stared at me for only an instant before he turned. "That woman is five months along." Then he was gone.

I went back to the kitchen, added some coal to the fire and sat by the window. What a crime this family had to live in this wild place. How long, six years? Everything was in years. Charlie had too many years of service to

Guarding the tunnels in winter was a dangerous assignment.

throw away, not enough to bid for a better job. It was the vicious seniority system again.

A sudden jangle of the phone startled me. It gave three short rings and two longer ones, the call for some section along the line. The ring came again; three short and two long. I took a lamp and went in the living room where the list of calls was tacked up beside the phone. Yes, that was the call for Troy. In the receiver I could hear a faint voice through the loud humming sound. "Troy section house? Hello?"

"This is Troy section," I shouted.

"This is Bill Fisher."

"Bill, where are you?"

"Oh, hello Kay-Kay. I'm at the summit. We're checking this line through. What are you doing at the Smith house?"

I told him about the storm and the children. "When will you be home?"

"Can't say. More trouble east of here. The fellows may need help. Listen, they are starting some flangers over the line, and an engine with a single coach to pick up and drop off tunnel guards. So be careful, and keep that new helper away from the tracks."

"All right." The room was suddenly bright with light. Upstairs the radio came on full blast. "Bill, the power just came on here."

"Good. I'll be home when I get there. Bye."

The whole Smith family had come stomping in. They all looked at me standing at the phone with a lamp in my hand and the lights burning.

"Millie, they were down there!" I cried.

She nodded thankfully, unable to get her breath, but her eyes spoke the relief in her heart. When little Rip sang, "Boy, no more school this winter," she smiled at their innocence. Charlie had no word to say.

"But where is Joe Kneebone?" I asked.

"Golly, I forgot about him, I was so glad to see the children. Charlie, he must still be out there."

"Bill's new helper," I explained. "He was with Millie."

Charlie Smith pulled on his ice-encrusted mackinaw. "Better get Millie to bed." He glanced at me anxiously as he pulled the door shut.

In twenty minutes or so I heard him on the porch again, stomping off the snow. Inside, he said, "I found your kid standin' by a tree, out of wind, his feet half-froze. He's gone to your outfit to dry out. That boy's got a lot to learn. How's Millie?"

"I've got her lying down in your bedroom. Charlie, I hope she is all right."

He nodded. His eyes told me that he was grateful, that there were no other words he could add to that.

Back at the outfit, after I got both stoves going full blast again, I fed Monday and fixed Joe a couple of sandwiches. He wanted milk to drink but I told him it was hot tea, coffee or water, period.

When Bill got home well after nine o'clock, tired and hungry, I fixed our dinner. After we'd piled into bed I lay thinking about the mountains, the snow, the war, the railroad. Somehow it seemed all worth it.

14. To Bed With Boots On

A faint gray light was seeping into the bedroom. Bill was sleeping soundly and no sound came from the other room. Then I heard a noise. "Bill, someone's at the door."

The knock came again. Bill growled in protest, got up and shuffled into the other room. I heard him tussle with the door and a Mexican voice, "Telephone want you, Meester."

He came back shivering and peered at his watch. "Holy smoke, it's nine o'clock. Wonder what happened to the alarm clock?"

"Nine? It couldn't be. It's still dark."

"Maybe we're having an eclipse." He dressed and left the room, telling Joe to get up. But in a minute he was back. "I gotta put on more clothes. There's six foot drifts out there. That's why it's dark in here."

I put on a robe and followed him to the kitchen door with Monday patting along behind. We stuck our noses out. "Monday," I cried, "we're snowed in!"

The outside world was a silent expanse of white. Bill had to plunge in to his waist to get to the sheds. Snow had drifted up to the windows of the baggage car. This was the end! Buried in the snow at the end of creation. Inside, the kitchen was freezing cold. Joe was standing at the sink in slippers and tousled hair, running the water.

"Easy on the water," I demanded. "The tanks must be nearly empty."

"Why, we are snowed in!"

"Well, it don't get hot."

"Of course not. There hasn't been a fire in the cookstove since yesterday."

"I can't wash then, I guess."

"A little cold water won't hurt you. Let's get some fires going in here."

"I think I better get a different job," he moaned. He ran a little water in the washpan and dabbled his fingers in it.

Experience had taught me that plenty of kerosene would make up for any skill I lacked in fire building. By the time Bill got back I had a steaming breakfast going and the new helper, having forgotten his discomfort, was on his first plate of hotcakes.

Bill came in, stomping off the snow, "I told the boss the rest of the cable would hold until spring. We move tomorrow morning; Emigrant Gap."

"Good! Why can't we move today?"

"It will take today to shovel these cars out, not to mention the Buick."

"I forgot all about the poor Buick. You mean we have to shovel these cars out by hand?"

"Sure, they'd jump the track with all that snow under them."

I glanced at Joe Kneebone. The word 'shovel' hadn't rung any bells. Bill took off his overshoes and pulled a chair up to the table. "Well, Joe, how was the breakfast?"

"Ain't through yet, but I'd say pretty good."

"We believe in eating," Bill said. "Nothing fancy but plenty of it."

"That's what I like," Joe replied.

"Good. As soon as you're through, start digging out the privie, then we'll begin on the outfit cars."

"Gee, I ain't got any clothes for snow."

"I know," Bill told him. "That's not my fault. There is a pair of boots and a raincoat in the tool car. Tomorrow we'll be in Emigrant Gap; you can buy some winter clothes there."

"But that takes money," Joe objected.

"Yeah, it does."

Joe went mournfully out to the tool car, came back with the boots and raincoat, but had to go back and close the end door. "Where's the shovel?"

"You might look in the tool car," Bill suggested. As he clumped back out again, Bill called, "Get a big one!"

"Bill, what changed his mind?" I asked. "He said he was going to quit."

"Breakfast. That was the best meal he's had since he left home. He'll be okay when he gets used to work."

The steady thumping of snowshovels against the baggage car continued all morning as Charlie Smith's crew helped the boys dig away the drifts. By noon the wheels and underparts of the 713 were visible. After lunch they dragged the motorcar up from Charlie's tool house and loaded it into our tool car. Then Bill and Joe headed down to dig out the Buick. It was after dark when they came plodding home. Bill flopped into a kitchen chair. "Damn the mountains," he panted. "Holy smoke, the dreamhouse has to be loaded yet."

"Tonight?"

"You know how early the local leaves Truckee." They ate and then went out in the dark to drag the frosted shanty and the electric wires into the tool car. When Bill finally came in he found me in bed with a lamp burning. He sat on the edge of the bed, took off his shoes, then picked up the alarm clock. "What a day. Let's see, five o'clock should be early enough."

"Will that give us time to have breakfast?"

"I think so." He rolled into bed. Then he sat up again. "How come you're so far down in the bed? Why, you've got your boots on!"

"I'll have you know I'm not rushing out of here in my slippers like I did in Truckee. Not in that snow."

"Oh, for gosh sake." Monday heard our voices and came scratching at the bedroom door. "Go to bed," Bill told him. "I'm having an argument with one member of the family; I don't want one with you."

Fatigue put Bill to sleep almost immediately, but I lay thinking about this rugged place, hiking down the mountain to the Buick, outfit cars and alarm clocks. I dreamed the 713 was in a long train. I was standing in the doorway looking at the snow out there. The train jerked and I stumbled because my feet were tangled in something. Bill, my feet! I awoke clawing at the covers twisted around my feet. Frightened and cold, I groped in the darkness for the bootjack. As the boots dropped on the floor my husband seemed to utter a grunt of satisfaction.

Bill was proud of himself the next morning. With fires going and coffee boiling, he'd started frying hotcakes. "See," he said, "the local hasn't showed up. We can take our time with breakfast."

I went out to the tool car for some eggs, just in time to hear a forbidding sound in the snowsheds; the shsss of a Westinghouse airbrake. I marched calmly back into the kitchen. "Hey, Farmer Jones, somebody is coupling an engine onto our tool car."

"What?" He jerked open the door. "Holy smoke, what did you guys do, get out before breakfast? Might as well get your coat, Kay. It's the local, all right." He jerked the steps into the kitchen and dropped them, snow and all, in front of the cupboard doors, put the coffee pot and griddle with two hot-cakes still on it into the oven, shut the dampers, blew out the table lamp and set it on the floor, leaving a wall lamp burning in each room. He stuck Monday in his box and said, stay there. By then I was standing in the doorway with flashlight poised. Outside, the snowy world was lighted by the grotesque rays of a headlight as I climbed down the ladder. Bill hollered to Joe sitting on the edge of the cot in his underwear, "All you have to do is ride along with the outfit. See that the doors don't swing open. But don't fall and get hurt." Then he dropped to the ground beside me.

There was a jerk as the 713 seemed to begrudge moving out of her snowy bed and go gliding off into the dark sheds. "There must be an easier way to make a living," Bill muttered.

The trail down the mountain was now only a mark in the deep drifts. Ahead of me the light of Bill's lantern swung crazily as he plowed along between the shrouded trees. My own flashlight pointed everywhere but the next hole I was stepping into, and the cold wet stuff filled my boots in the first few yards. I was lucky, I suppose, that we were going down instead of up and my husband was breaking trail ahead. He was lucky too; if he'd said one word I was ready to tell him what I thought of outfit cars.

We arrived an hour later at some snowbound hamlet. There were a few houses and a store, their occupants sleeping peacefully. I could hear a freight blasting its way up the mountain. Bill parked against a snowbank. "Only couple of hundred yards up to the track. The outfit should be here by now."

I pulled on wet stockings, struggled into clammy boots and we started walking, finally reaching a small telephone shack beside the tracks. We stomped into the bare shack and hopefully touched the rusty stove. Like my poor feet, it was stone cold. Bill peered into the darkness. "No outfits," he announced.

"Wonderful! What do we do now?"

"Find out what's happened. Telegraph office here, right down the track."

For a moment I thought he was going to start down the track and leave me to freeze to death, but he turned to a phone on the wall. And to make things a little crazier, a cordial feminine voice answered.

"This is Fisher up at the spur. Can you tell me where the local is?"

"Why the local is gone." I could hear her excited voice plainly. "Was that your outfit they were supposed to leave here?"

"Supposed to? Didn't they leave it?"

"They carried it by. They were to pick up a bad order car of ammunition off the siding and didn't do that either."

"My wife is here with me, and we haven't even had breakfast. What's the matter with those guys?" Bill was getting mad.

"They'll have to clear Eighty-seven at Knapp or Midas so they'll probably call in, and then we'll find out. Mr. Fisher, bring your wife down to the office. I have a warm fire and coffee."

"Okay. Thanks." He hung up the receiver.

"How far is it? Just a step, I suppose."

"Only quarter of a mile."

"Bill, I don't know what you expect of me! I'm nearly frozen and you want to go tromping off again."

"Nothing to build a fire with here. We'd better go down there."

With flashlight swinging, we started out, Bill tramping ahead between the rails where the snow was frozen solid. Things seemed to be getting whiter, then I realized it was the first gray streaks of dawn. We went through a short section of snowshed. Lights ahead disclosed a narrow tiny building crammed between the two tracks. Inside, odors of coal smoke, pine oil and fresh coffee greeted us. An elderly woman was typing, headphone clamped to her ear. The small overheated office held a telegraph table, some kind of switchboard and a pot-bellied stove topped by a steaming coffee pot. The woman swung around in her swivel chair.

The little telegraph office at Emigrant Gap.   *(Robert DelCarlo photo)*

"You poor girl," she declared, "you look like an icicle. If that fellow Slate knew what he was doing to you . . . but he wouldn't care. I've known him for years and he's nothing but an ornery cuss. I made the coffee strong so it would warm you up."

My husband pulled a chair near the stove, helped me get the boots off and poured coffee into two mugs. She'd made it strong all right. I held my feet toward the radiant stove. Bill said, "You're Mrs. Merrithew, aren't you? We sure appreciate this. We walked out of Troy this morning . . ."

Mrs. Merrithew was smiling but suddenly she whirled in her chair as a phone bell jangled. "Yes . . . Is this Slate? . . . At Blue Canyon you say? . . . Didn't you have a message on that ammunition car here? . . . The dispatcher is hopping mad, and what about those outfits? . . . Hello? . . . He hung up on me, the stinker!"

I said, "What about our outfits?"

"He's bringing them back, but only because he forgot the bad order car. He'll have to crossover and back up the eastbound track. And he wants me to cover up for him, mind you." A westbound passenger roared by. She got up to read its number, looked at her fire, and plumped back in her chair.

Like this dingy office, she was worn thin by the countless trains. I noticed her out-of-style hair, the laced leather boots of a past era. I wondered how many decades she had carried that brown satchel on the floor beside her chair.

I looked again at the open satchel. It contained knitting on wooden needles and something that looked like the butt of a pistol!

She turned to her phone again. "O S Emigrant Gap. Number Eighty-seven, eight seven, no signals, by at 712, seven one two AM. Say, the local is not by. He called from the lower switch to say he's coming back up to get that car off the siding . . . That's right." She put down her phone disgustedly.

"How long have you worked for the railroad?" I asked, ready for the usual ten or twenty year figure.

She looked as if I were too young to ask such a question. "Longer than I want to admit," she answered. "Thirty-five years."

"Thirty-five years?"

"You walked out of Troy this morning, Mrs. Fisher? Well, I went to Troy as a bride. My husband was staff operator there for six years. In those days you worked twelve hour shifts, seven days a week."

"You were there that long?" I exclaimed. "How did you pass the time?"

"I was young, and I spent a lot of time in the office with my husband. I learned telegraphy from being around it so much. After a year or so I took the job of night operator, but Paul kept the day shift. He had the most seniority!"

There was a respectful silence from the Fisher family. The telegraph instruments clicked away. Then a buzzer sounded. She whirled in her chair.

"There is your local coming," she announced. "I'll stop them here and you can just ride up in your outfit."

I didn't quite expect to see our tool car backing up the track, followed by the baggage car and a caboose. Conductor Slate was on the caboose steps glowering at Mrs. Merrithew's stop signal. The train jerked to a halt with the 713 right beside us.

"Mrs. Merrithew," I said, "thanks for being so kind to us. I'll come to visit you when the weather is better. I'd like to hear what happened to your husband."

She put her hand on my arm. "Just call me Edith. My dear, he died of a rattlesnake bite in '27."

Bill helped me up the ladder into the 713. "Better sit down. Man, it looks like a tornado struck the place." There was a strong odor of sourdough, the floor was a lake where snow had melted off the steps. In the living room a figure stirred among the blankets on the steel cot. Under the cot, huddling wide-eyed, was Monday.

"You poor dog," I cried. "Bill, he's scared to death."

The train started to move. Joe raised up, bleary-eyed. "Where are we?"

"Aw, skip it," Bill said. He came back and sat down with the dog in his arms.

It was eight-thirty. My boots were still wet and clammy. I looked at the undulating lake of water on the kitchen floor. I felt hungry and tired. "Bill, when can we bid off this job?"

"In the spring, maybe."

*The outfit car parked
at Emigrant Gap,
dreamhouse on the right.*

I can't imagine a more violent end than freezing to death with my pants down, and I was expecting that gruesome fate any minute.

The dreamhouse in a storm! Howling wind sifted snow through the cracks, the narrow walls shook from the force of the gale. What if it upset with me inside? Why in heaven's name were we still in Emigrant Gap after three weeks? Another gust of wind struck and the roof departed with a roar, leaving me staring up at a blizzard pouring down pillows of snow.

"Bill!" I screamed. Through the door crack I saw Joe Kneebone's head peer out of the tool car. He stumbled down the steps in heroic haste.

"The roof is gone!" I yelled.

The snowy board was slid into place above me and the blizzard cut off, but it was too late to consider staying. My only thought was to hide my embarrassment as I waded back to the outfit, and who should come tramping through the snow but my dear husband, the inspiration of pioneers. He turned his back to the wind, stared at the fury in my eyes and the snow in my hair. "What happened?"

"Why don't you ask him?" I shouted. Joe was standing in the snow with upstretched hands holding down the vibrating roof of the dreamhouse.

From the safety of the warm living room I watched them dig out some boulders to place on the flapping lid. With the situation well in hand, my husband meandered into the outfit grinning. "That must have been quite a surprise."

"Bill Fisher, I'll have you know it wasn't funny! If you think I'm going to

134

Cleanup work. Rotary plow waiting "in the clear" at Emigrant Gap.

put up with this any longer . . .If you don't get me out of these mountains you can just stay in this damned outfit and . . ."

"You're just excited, Kay-Kay."

"Well, how do you think I felt with that guy holding the roof down for me?" Monday came over to take my side. "I'm a woman, remember."

"We are moving to Colfax day after tomorrow."

"Is that out of the snow?"

"Practically."

I'd heard that before. But after I'd cooled down he insisted Colfax was below the snow level because it was two thousand feet lower in altitude. He apologized and assumed full responsibility. Ordinarily, he explained, we wouldn't be up here this time of year. We were supposed to work in the lower altitudes in winter and in the mountains in summertime. But things were sort of mixed up.

To me that didn't justify sleeping in a frigid bedroom and fighting that ungodly dreamhouse every day. And I found out later that every repair gang did their summer work amid December snows and finished the low altitude winter jobs in the heat of July. It was standard practice; it would never happen again, but always did.

But there *was* a war on.

In spite of the storms a steady stream of trains went by loaded with tanks and army trucks, flat cars full of a new gadget called jeeps. There were special trains crammed with soldiers and sailors, some waving, some just looking sad, all of them pathetically young. News reports became urgent. Our vocabulary acquired new words; censorship, draftee, G.I., camouflage, rationing. All of which may have justified us being up here but didn't make living in the 713 any more cheerful.

Each passing train would throw frozen snow against the outfit so Bill had to board up the windows on one side to keep them from being broken. Then there were the flangers; fast running engines with snowplows that could slam the packed white stuff with such force it made the old baggage car rock and bring you straight up in bed wondering if there was a train wreck. Between times the big rotary plows throwing arching plumes of snow blasted their shrill frightening whistle as they passed.

To help matters along we ran out of coal. Running out of coal, my husband explained, usually meant hauling a new supply from some convenient storage bunker with the motorcar but now they couldn't use the motorcar so they had to carry it in sacks whenever they could. Every time they dumped a sack the lumps would rattle discouragingly in the empty bin. "For gosh sake," Bill said, "we can't even get ahead of you."

So I froze for three days while they tried to get ahead of me.

And then there was laundry. With no washing facility within thirty miles and Bill wearing so much heavy clothing, I couldn't keep it all washed, and trying to dry it meant using more coal. It was useless to carry hot water out to the cement wash tubs in the frigid tool car so I washed the small things in the kitchen sink and the heavy clothing with a tub and scrub board balanced on a box in the middle of the kitchen. The old bell cord running through the outfit became permanently adorned with wool shirts and underwear. Bill hated wet clothes hitting him in the face but he didn't mention it.

And the matter of shopping. The local store sold canned goods, bread, meat (sometimes), fishing tackle, hip boots, anti-freeze, in fact everything but what you went down there for. One thing you could be sure of, the price would be high and that was important with Joe Kneebone.

Last but not least, we did not move out 'day after tomorrow'; we were still in Emigrant Gap after another week went past, but the storm had abated.

"Is that sunshine?" Bill asked, finishing breakfast.

I pried open the frozen door. "Why, it's a beautiful morning! Come and look." The sun was breaking over a mountain I hadn't seen before. Beyond a canyon full of silent trees in white overcoats, it lay like a huge mound of glistening sugar. Up and down the tracks there was no sign of life but the plume of smoke rising from our tin stovepipe. The 713 was shrouded in six-foot-long icicles gleaming in the sunlight.

"Is that sunshine?"

We both stood in the doorway admiring the silent majestic display of nature's handiwork. Majestic, yes, if the living things on her slopes could survive her onslaughts to create it. We turned back to the breakfast table to finish our coffee.

"Can't use the motorcar today," Bill observed. "I'll go down to the station and phone; see what the boss has in mind."

"I'll walk with you. I need some fresh air."

Leaving Joe to straighten up in the tool car, we set off crunching along on the hard snow, Monday trotting happily ahead. The track men were gathered around their toolhouse, getting shovels and snow brooms ready. Bill spoke and they grinned, accepting us as just some more poor railroaders who'd lost their marbles. At the little office Mrs. Merrithew insisted I have some of her strong coffee.

She had been wonderful company the past three weeks. I hadn't realized my trips to visit her were quite an achievement. Slowly but surely I was getting to be a pioneer like that Bill Fisher.

The motherly operator had told me much about the workings of a teeming railroad. Her chattering instruments carried a constant stream of orders to trains, instructions to various officials, reports of trouble. Phones had replaced much of the telegraphing but the instruments were still busy and, she said, still the most reliable.

I learned that most of the eastbound freights coming upgrade from Colfax had five engines. Those trains all stopped west of her office where two of the smaller engines would be uncoupled, the tenders of the big Mallets filled with water, and the crews went to eat. There were two eating houses, one at each end of the yard which she referred to as the 'upper and lower cook cars'. There was an extra track between the main lines and often it too, would be blocked with a freight train while its crew was eating.

The smaller 'Colfax helpers', as she called them, each came up to her office where she gave them permission to switch over and be ready to return west. She gave each a written clearance and any orders that applied, handing them up to the fireman by means of wooden hoops with the 'flimsies' clipped to them. Each order had previously been copied as dictated by the dispatcher, and she repeated back each order and clearance, carefully spelling out the times shown.

Sometimes she had orders for westbound freights or passenger trains. These she clipped to wooden hoops and then climbed a slender ladder fastened to an iron post, setting the sticks into sockets so the train crew could reach out and catch them. As the trains rolled by, the little office would shake violently but she'd go right on tapping out a message with her telegraph key while she noted the number of a passing engine, or answer a phone call from track men wanting a 'line-up' of trains in her area. She wrote down the number and time of each train that clattered past her little station on a form she called 'the train sheet'.

Between trains she told me of bygone days when the railroad was the only way in and out of this wild area. She had started carrying her pistol after her husband died. "I've really only fired it at stumps," she assured me, "but it gives me a comfortable feeling."

"Do you know Parson Woods?" I asked her one day.

"Do I! He was quite smitten on me after I became a widow. I had a riding mare and he would carry the bales of hay up to my little barn when the local put them off. I was very thrilled." She laughed and patted my arm. "Once he fell on some ice with one of those bales and that was the end of our romance."

On one visit all tracks were blocked by stalled trains, the office crowded with officials bawling into phones and papers strewn on the floor. I gathered there was a derailment, a car tipped over and tracks torn out. It was all several miles away but her office was the nearest point of communication. I didn't stay, but remembered how the officials looked as if they belonged to the railroad and nowhere else. They all wore suits, the official badge of authority, and I wondered how they could keep looking so clean riding those smoky engines.

Bill had finished on the phone and indicated we were ready to go. He held

"Sometimes both tracks would be blocked by trains."
(Original photo taken at Emigrant Gap in 1942 by Gordon S. Campbell of Elko, Nevada)

my hand going through the short section of snowshed because of the black ice. "Well, I got unpleasant news. Norden for two weeks."

"Oh, no! Madge said it was the worst place in the world."

"Like Siberia this time of year," he agreed. "The outfits will be parked inside the sheds. The boss said to send Joe down to the signal gang in Roseville, and me be ready to move tomorrow. Kay, how about you going down and stay with your aunt for a week or so?"

"And leave you to batch alone?"

"Won't be bad for me. There is a trainmen's eating shack at Norden, less than a quarter mile from the spur. I'll only have to make breakfast. I can get plenty of leftovers from the cookshack for the dog, and fix a little house in the tool car, put up some steps, leave the door ajar. He'll be lonesome but he'll make out all right."

We walked in silence.

"Kay-Kay, you need a vacation from all this; you've had a rough time. Let's go down to the store and phone your aunt right now. If it's okay, you can catch the train here tonight. I'll send Joe in on the same train."

Aunty was all in favor of my coming. During the day the boys loaded the motorcar, drained the hoses after filling the tanks and then rolled them up in the tool car. Bill decided to leave the light wires and dreamhouse until morning.

That evening he called the dispatcher for a close figure on No. 21 and filed a stop order for the train, so we wouldn't be waiting out in the cold. He specified 'outfit', hoping to avoid a long walk. It was past our normal bedtime when the headlight came in sight of us standing in the snow. Bill blinked his light once and the engineer answered with a single "wowt". A long string of mail cars drifted by us, clouds of steam rising from the train heat vents. Then a coach and brakeman standing on the steps with a light, stopped only a few yards away.

Joe climbed on first, naturally. Bill handed my suitcase to the brakeman and hugged me tightly. "Don't worry about a thing," he said. "Just relax and have a good time."

I found a seat in the dim coach, saw the lights of the little telegraph office slip by outside, and settled back. Would we ever get out of that 713? There were better paying jobs in shipyards and war plants now. The government had frozen wages and railroaders were on the low end. But I knew that whatever his purpose in hanging on, I had a kind, thoughtful husband. I dozed off thinking of Dad Letterman's counsel; "You got to make up your mind to staying together."

15. Decision By Two

I was standing in line at a ticket window. My aunt and her children were at my elbow, the youngsters wide-eyed at the bustle in the huge station and the booming voice announcing trains. People were crowding toward the iron gates, service men kissing anxious wives, Red Caps wheeling carts of baggage.

"I'm taking Twenty-eight to Norden," I told the pale-looking clerk. "I have a pass."

"Norden is not a stop for Number Twenty-eight, madam. You'll have to take Number Two-ten tonight."

"Norden is a stop for all trains," I argued. "They cut helpers there."

He looked at me blankly. "Helpers?"

"Helper engines," I said impatiently. "They can't cut off a helper without stopping, can they?"

The clerk glared at me, his finger indicating a spot on the big schedule under the counter glass. "Norden is not a passenger stop for Twenty-eight." Next, please?"

"Come on, Aunty." I picked up my suitcase and marched to the gate marked Track Six.

"But Kay," she fretted, "are you sure? What if they don't let you get off? Maybe you'd better come home with us and take that night train."

"I wired Bill I'd be on this train," I insisted, "and I will be." At the gate I approached the stationmaster, showing him my pass. "I want to get off Twenty-eight when they cut their helper at Norden."

The gold braid on his sleeve gleamed. "Just tell the porter you are dead-heading," he smiled, waving me through. "Barnes is your conductor."

"Thank you. My Aunt would like to see me off."

He nodded and waved us all through.

"I'm surprised, Kay," Aunty said as we hurried between the waiting coaches. "How did you know all that?"

"Aunty, I've learned a lot these past months!"

Yes, I had learned more than she would ever understand. The fact I was on a pass and knew what a helper engine was told the stationmaster that I was an employee's wife. The porter hardly glanced at my pass. I talked to Aunty for a minute and kissed the children, then climbed aboard.

As the train moved out of the station I peered out for a last sight of the teeming city. I was headed back to the mountains, to my husband and the 713. I wondered how Norden could be worse than Troy. Surely it couldn't be. When we stopped at Roseville to couple on the helper, I thought about Aunty's parting remarks. "Kay, you can't go on living in that railroad car. Bill should be able to provide something better. Couldn't he go into defense work, like Vicki's husband?"

Bill was doing defense work now. The railroad had to run, and it had to have experienced men. But why did we have to go living in that dingy old baggage car? Because of seniority; the age-old rule that length of service came before ability. Like an oak tree, it grew slowly.

It was long after dark when the train began slowing down. From the sounds and dim lights silhouetting the great beams marching past outside, I knew we had entered some snowsheds. Conductor Barnes came along, and said, "Norden, Mrs. Fisher. Do you have someone meeting you?"

"Yes, my husband. Thanks for being so considerate."

In the coach vestibule a porter was opening the steps, the tracks widened to disclose a telegraph office and some men watching the train come in. Steam and smoke clouded the darkness but I recognized my husband. "Bill! Hello, dear," I called.

"Hiya, wife," he answered, walking alongside the train until the cars stopped.

Conductor Barnes handed Bill my suitcase. "Careful when you step down," he said. "Icy footing out there."

Bill put the suitcase down and took me in his arms. "Glad to see you, Kay-Kay. It's been lonesome up here."

"You poor thing. Gee, it's cold. Why, it's raining."

"No, that's snow melting on top of the sheds. Worse than rain. I brought your boots. Let's go in the office where you can put them on."

We entered an area almost filled with an immense coal stove and several caboose chairs, but the brightly lighted room was like nothing I'd seen before. It was quite long and all the left side was taken by a high counter-like arrangement. Above that was a large plaque marked with white lines and dozens of small lights, like a flat Christmas tree. A baldheaded man with glasses and a fringe of white hair was pulling and pushing some handles, a long row of them that stuck out of the front of the high counter. Behind him, against the other wall, was a desk with a shaded lamp, scattered papers, phones and chattering telegraph instruments.

"This is an amazing place," Bill said. "That's Ralph Duncan. He's switching the helper off your train by remote control."

"What are all those handles for?" I wondered. Mr. Duncan had just pushed one and pulled another. It looked very complicated.

"That's a Saxby-Farmer Interlocker, and it sure is interesting. All the switches around here are operated from this machine," Bill explained. "See, he's just cleared Twenty-eight to go." Outside the window my train was moving, the dining car went by, then the Pullmans with two red lights on the last one disappeared into the dark sheds. "There on the model board," Bill went on. "Those lights are Twenty-eight leaving. That light is the helper on the siding. This stuff is all maintained by the signal department." Mr. Duncan was now on the phone but Bill caught his eye and motioned at us. The operator waved. "You even have to get an OK to walk in this place!" Bill explained.

Outside he put a raincoat over my shoulders; the dirty drops of water were almost a downpour, splashing on the black ice covering the ground. Icicles hung like stalactites from the timbers overhead. We walked between icy rails through the ghostly tunnel-like sheds. Bill had the trainman's lantern and a flashlight for me. Then we came to a huge cavern and a big throbbing locomotive, steam curling over its machinery.

"Turntable," Bill said above the noise. "He's turning around to go back to Roseville." The engine was actually moving in a circle, like a toy train. Then the bridge-like structure halted and the great engine came slowly to life, its massive wheels clumping off into a shed passageway. We walked on, following more frosty railroad tracks.

"Bill, this is a terrible place. How far is the outfit?"

"Quite a ways yet."

The 713 stood on a track branching off into a dark cubicle of snowshed. There was no sign of life, no view, no sound except the constant dripping of dirty water. Bill located the steps with his light and kicked off something that looked like white gravel. "Rock salt," he explained. "Keeps ice off the steps." He pushed open the door and Monday met us, yapping and wiggling all over.

"Oh, Monday," I cried. "I'll bet you've been lonesome for me." He licked my hand and ran around in circles, yapping Let's get out of here! Tell this Bill Fisher to get us out of here!

The outfit was warm and dry but a ghostly feeling of isolation surrounded me. We must be a half-mile from the nearest habitation. Bill explained the Buick was parked above us on the highway but I couldn't reach it without walking through the sheds, and he didn't want me to attempt that alone here.

"Did you have a good visit?" Bill asked. "How is Vicki?"

"They moved to Los Angeles. Aunty said Jack is making lots of money but they aren't getting along very well."

He took me in his arms. "It's going to be rough for you here, but I'm hoping to get out in a week or so. At least we'll have privacy until I get a helper again."

The privacy didn't seem to produce expected results. Bill came home the next day tired, dirty and disgusted. For me it had been like a day in jail, with lights burning all day because the snowsheds were like a wet dark tunnel. I couldn't go outside for fear of the trains that clattered past only a few feet away. Some stopped for long periods while helpers were being uncoupled. Then the snowsheds would be completely blocked off and I couldn't even see daylight sifting through the cracks of the timbers. I could get only a few weak programs on the radio. With all this I was fit to be tied in about three days. By the end of a week I was definitely getting stir-crazy.

Saturday Bill promised to be in early. We'd walk up to the Buick and go to a town, some place where we could have dinner and dance, stay in a motel. But that night when he didn't get in by six o'clock I began to worry about what had happened to him. Around eight I took off my dress and made a sandwich. It was weird being alone in the outfit, without knowing. By ten o'clock I was frantic. Midnight found me in bed, frightened and crying. Where was he? Could he have been hurt? I tried to sleep but it was impossible.

Sometime later I heard a freight train pull in and stop. Maybe the crew had seen him or knew what happened. Maybe I could get to the station and find out. I got up, pulled on warm clothes and boots, found the flashlight.

I crept down the ice steps and started walking along between the train and the snowshed, stumbling against the dripping cars and black timbers. Ahead I could hear the heavy throbbing sound of air pumps on the locomotive. Then I came to the hot cylinders with whisps of steam drifting upward, and barely enough space for me to pass between them and the shed posts. The massive rods and wheels, higher than my head, looked frightening only two feet away from me in the flashlight beam. I inched past another set of cylinders and more drive wheels, and finally reached the front end. High above me I could see a figure in the dim cab.

"Hey, up there!" I pointed the flashlight up at him.

The figure came to life and peered down. Then he grabbed a light and came swinging down the iron ladder. "What in hell you doing here in the middle of the night, lady?"

I could hardly distinguish his face in the noisy darkness. "My husband hasn't come home and I'm worried about him. He's a signalman. Have you seen him?"

"Who? You better go home, lady. Where do you live?"

"In that outfit back there on the spur."

"Oh! Yeah, we did see a guy this side of Andover. He had a motorcar set off in the snow, looked like he'd been stuck. That him?"

"Maybe it was. Was he all right?"

"Looked okay. I wouldn't worry, lady. He probably followed us in all right after we cleaned the rail. If he did, he'd make it down the siding around us, once we got in the sheds."

"Well . . . thanks."

He put a gloved hand on my arm. "You go back to your outfit. I'll hold this train long enough for you to get there. Now take it careful."

I nodded and turned back in the blackness beside the big locomotive, still not sure, still alone. Tears poured down my face. Suddenly there was a light flashing at me.

"Kay! What are you doing out here? I was half nuts when I found you gone."

"Bill!" I sobbed. "I . . . I was looking for you . . ."

He took my hand and pulled me along "But why did you come out here? You could get killed. These sheds are dangerous at night."

I jerked my hand away. "What did you expect of me? Why didn't you send some word you'd be late?"

He grabbed and half-carried me along until we reached the outfit car. Inside he pulled off his wet coat and turned to getting a fire going, slamming the coal into the pot-bellied heater.

"Well, what did happen to you?" I cried.

He tried to be patient. "It was one of those things. They called me to help change out a burned transformer this afternoon, twelve miles from here. After I'd started home I couldn't remember if we'd turned the power back on. The signals would all go out of commission. I went all the way back to check."

"What time was that?"

"About six. But then it started snowing and I couldn't make it on the motorcar. I was too far from any phone. Decided to wait for a train to clear the track but nothing came for three hours. Should have just started walking. But why did you go out like that alone?"

"Was I supposed to stay in this . . . this outfit all night alone, wondering if you were dead? Bill, I'm not going to live like a mole on this crazy railroad! If you want to stay here . . ."

"Let's go to bed."

It was past noon Sunday when we awakened. Bill had tossed most of the night and I'd heard every train come and go. In the dim cold outfit car there was nothing but the clock to indicate it was daylight outside.

After a silent breakfast Bill said he would walk down to the station to check for mail. It was still snowing; no use trying to go anywhere now. I tried to apologize for what I'd done but he didn't want to talk about it. He put on his coat and left. I went to the tool car and brought our dog in to give him some breakfast, then I stoked up the heater and pulled a caboose chair up to it. Monday curled up at my feet.

What was the answer? Why were we living here at the very end of creation? It was foolish for him to keep working like this, waiting for someone to die before he could get a better job. He would either have to quit—or I would. Seniority. I hated it.

It seemed to be hours before I heard him at the door. He came in and tossed some mail on the desk, then hung up his coat.

"Kay-Kay, I've decided to quit. There is no use going on like this with you unhappy. I don't mind this damn outfit because I get out during the day and work with the other guys, but you're stuck in this hole . . ."

"Well . . ." I began. I'd expected some argument to my own decision but now he'd made the same choice. I knew he liked the railroad and believed in staying with it. He could wait out the seniority system. But not alone.

"That's the only answer," he declared, and walked off into the kitchen. I heard him pour coal into the cookstove, banging the lids noisily, but he didn't come back to the living room.

I looked at the mail he'd brought. There was a letter from cousin Vicki: "*Dear Kay: I want you to know first. Jack has left me—.*" She had written something and crossed it out. "*I guess it was my fault for prodding him into a big money money job. He didn't like it and he started drinking. I—.*" More was crossed out. "*I guess I've lost my home and marriage and everything. I couldn't go back to him now . . .*" I threw the letter into the coal bucket and went into the kitchen where Bill was standing beside the stove.

"Dear," I said, "don't quit your job."

"Why not?"

"I don't want you to."

"Why?"

"I don't know why. Just don't." Monday came in and wiggled between our feet. On the roof the dismal dripping started again. The lights flickered. I said, "Dear, go in and get the best program you can on the radio. Turn on all the lights we have, and light the lamps too. I'll whip up a good dinner. We'll stick it out together."

"Here in this lousy outfit car?"

"If that's what it takes — yes!"

16. Yellow Is For Spring

The episode at Norden did something to us. It drew us closer together. It showed us that marriage is what you make it, and it proved that the ways of the railroad and wandering of the 713 would always be unpredictable. I doubt if the experience changed the old car any, except to start her roof leaking. In a few days Bill had a telegram when he came home.

"Truckee, tomorrow," he announced.

It was almost spring in Truckee. The rail-laying gangs were starting in the mountains. First thing I did was to visit Emma, wonder at how much lower her voice had become, and hear news of Dora Terroli. We got a new helper, a young redheaded kid named Bob. Mr. Candy was with us again. His teeth were larger and straighter than ever.

One day I gave him a ride to town in the Buick. He appreciated my friendliness so much, and wanted to pay me.

"No, no," I said, sliding out of the car. "You do me many favors."

"Oh, si, senora." We were on the sidewalk, he was trying to slip a silver dollar into my pocket. "Un peso, senora. You buy chocolatay." I hurried down the street, with him following. Then suddenly he wasn't there. When I looked back he was being held firmly at the back of the neck by the long arm of Constable Slate.

"Oh, Mr. Candy!" I hurried to rescue him but Mr. Slate glowered at me.

"Last time this Mex was in trouble," he said menacingly, "you stuck up for him. What's the connection?"

"I'll have you know he's just a friend. He didn't do anything."

"He was chasing a dame down the street."

"The 'dame' was me. He was only trying to give me some money."

"Money for what?" He looked me over.

The people of Truckee may have remembered that I once pulled Dora Terroli through their midst, now they would place me as the woman who stood and shouted at Constable Slate. I threatened to slap his face and even have him arrested. Poor Mr. Candy suffered the most, he nearly died of embarrassment.

From Truckee to Boca, a sleepy station where the trains roared by at fifty miles an hour. No. 210 arrived there just about breakfast time and often we could see the passengers eating in the dining car not six feet from our window.

One morning I'd run out of coffee but told Bill not to get concerned; No. 210 would be along in a minute. When the train drew to a stop I tapped on the chef's door with my broom handle. A white-hatted cook looked out.

"Good morning. I'd like to borrow a pound of coffee," I told him.

He ducked back in amazement and returned with a paper sack, handing it to me across the open space. "Now Ah has seen everything, lady," he said as his train began to move.

"Thanks," I called. "Let me know if I can help you sometime."

An eighty-mile jump the first of May, back over the summit to a place called Gold Run. Driving over we stopped to visit Millie Smith. The snow had melted enough so the steep twisting road between the tall firs was open all the way to her house. Since it was Saturday the kids were home and they all came running out excitedly.

"Missus Kay!" Summie greeted. "We got a new baby sister and we named it for you."

In the living room they all crowded around while I held their darling little girl. Millie explained, "The children wanted me to name her after you, but golly, Charlie's always been awantin' to give my name to one of our girls. So . . . well, it turned out she is Mildred Kay Smith."

"Millie, I'm thrilled! I don't know what to say. But I'm afraid she won't have black hair like mine."

"That's all right," Summie assured me. "We like her just the same."

Sipping coffee around the kitchen table Millie said there was almost a sure chance Charlie would be able to bid out of Troy before the summer was over. Going back down to the highway I hardly felt the rocks and bumps. What a lovable family. How great it was to have them for friends.

We were to join the track gang at Gold Run, but when we got there the long string of cars seemed to occupy all the available trackage. Bill called it the 'oil siding' on kind of a knoll above the main lines. The only space left was on a steep grade. I could picture us hiking up to the kitchen and sliding down to the bedroom. The work train with our cars didn't arrive until after five o'clock, and Bill had fretted for two hours about the problem, but the day was saved when we found "Sailor" Reagan was the conductor.

"Don't you worry, young fella," he told Bill. "We'll put you up on the sandhouse spur. They'll squawk and chew me about the switching overtime, but I got enough whiskers to get by with it."

So I learned that "whiskers" meant seniority. Mr. Reagan had forty years and Bill didn't have enough to even show! But the location was great. When the cars were finally spotted, our back door looked out at tall pine trees and a dirt road that led fifty yards to the main highway. A grocery store, postoffice, and garage were within easy walking distance. The other door faced two main lines and two sidings a hundred feet away, and the grade here was nearly level so the eastbound trains didn't rock the outfit. Westbound freights all stopped to cool wheels while the crews made a walking inspection of their train. It was like having our own private track — except for the helper living with us.

One evening we took a walk up the track, Bill, Monday and I. The railroad was on a high ridge and the scarred land fell away from high cliffs on each side. Bill explained that years ago it had all been cut away by hydraulic mining operations. Many millions in gold had been taken out of the "Stewart diggings" on the east side and the Dutch Flat area to the north. The railroad prevented the miners from taking out the ground occupied by the tracks.

"There is probably a million dollars in gold still here," Bill said. But it was a hundred feet beneath us and quite unobtainable.

I liked Gold Run, but it was typical that we stayed only a few days in the pleasant spots and weeks in locations like Troy and Corral Track Five.

"Don't plant a garden," Bill announced that week-end. "The Towle maintainer will be following the rail gang next week and we are going to a signal repair job west of Colfax. We'll be moving Tuesday."

"We'll be in the west end of the yard," Bill explained as we drove into the town of Colfax with its two-block main street facing the railroad, like Truckee. There was a nice looking station, but standard railroad color, and its train-order signal like a tall tree with only two arms. An engine was moving some refrigerator cars alongside a fruit packing warehouse.

Colfax, California in 1941. NCNGRR track at far left.   *(From a postcard)*

A quarter mile farther on, the yards widened out to six tracks. On the last one, near a hillside covered with fruit trees, stood the good old 713 and 787. Bill said there would be no problem getting lights and we might be able to run the refrigerator.

What a wonderful relief from the months of cold snow and snowsheds. Monday loved the trees and immediately began planting a new bone yard. The weather was warm, almost hot. We were doing our winter work in the summertime.

We were all alone in the 'west end'; no other cars or outfits. The mainline was several tracks away and even so, the trains coming from Roseville coasted into town, slowing for their stop at the water columns. Westbound trains drifted downgrade with only a moderate clickety-clack as they headed for the valley. In a few days it was actually a little lonely. I missed the crashing sounds we'd known up in the mountains. Of course, Monday and I drove uptown every day to shop. What an advantage not to worry about stocking food ahead for a couple of weeks or more.

"Hey, look outside," Bill said one morning. "We have company. They must have come in during the night."

When I opened the door toward the mainline I was met by a wall of flowers. Geraniums, bushes of them! They stood in pots along the deck of a red-painted tank car. Coupled to it was an ancient coach and several more outfit cars. A lady in a quilted robe came out onto the porch of the coach. She was short and slender, her hair turning grey, but she had a pleasant face.

"Hello," I called. "Nice to have neighbors. What outfit are you?"

"We're the Sealy's," she answered cordially. "We're the painting gang."

That was a surprise. I didn't know the railroad ever painted anything. "What are you going to paint in Colfax?" I queried.

"Mike paints everything he comes to," she told me simply. "I guess he'll be starting on your outfit cars this morning."

Surprise number two! "You mean he'll paint my kitchen for me?"

Bill said behind me, "Kay, they paint only the outside of outfit cars."

"If you want to do your kitchen," Mrs. Sealy replied, "I'm sure Mike will give you the paint. You can do it on your own."

"Well, thanks," I told her. "I love your geraniums!"

Breakfast was hardly over when things began to bustle around the 713. Mike Sealy knocked on the door and made himself acquainted. He said his men would start spraying as soon as I was ready, and if I had some newspapers they'd cover the windows for me. I gathered that otherwise they would paint right over them. He suggested I visit his wife while the work was in progress. He was a small, nervous man in red-smeared overalls and painter's cap. He carried an unlighted brown cigarette in the corner of his mouth.

Mrs. Sealy was eating breakfast alone when I went over, and I noticed she was drinking a Coke instead of coffee. She insisted I bring Monday inside so he wouldn't get into the paint, then she opened another Coke for me.

"Don't you eat with your husband?" I asked.

"Oh, no. He has five men so we have a boarding outfiit with a cook. Mike gets his meals free for managing the boarding car so I eat alone. The arrangement doesn't include me."

Another example, I thought, of the wondrous ways of the railroad. She evidently lived on Cokes, judging from the three cases of empty bottles in one corner of the kitchen.

Her car was arranged like ours but there were no side doors. You entered directly into the kitchen; the only other door being on the opposite end in the bedroom. It was much lighter because of all the windows and clean gray paint but the ceiling was the same domed shape. Remembering Madge's comments about coaches, I could see how so many windows cut down privacy and served to remind you it was just a worn-out railroad car.

"Your outfit's all done," Mr. Sealy reported at noon. "Looks like a brand new car. Careful when you go up the steps."

Monday and I went out to look. The 713 resembled something out of a movie as it sparkled in its resplendent new coat of red. They had painted the wheels, part of the track, and one window where the paper has slipped.

"Don't you have anything but red?" I asked him.

"Got yellow, and brown," he replied, "but we can't use them on outfits."

"Railroads are obstinate things," I commented, leaving him disappointed.

Helen Sealy and her husband left a week later and I was alone again in the remote corner of the yards. But May was well along, wild flowers were blooming among the stacks of ties, I began to get spring-cleaning fever. Mike had left me two gallons of inside gray paint so I persuaded Bill to mix it with a gallon of white he had in the tool car and let me start on the kitchen.

"You'll break your neck," he grumbled, but he did help by cleaning the domed ceiling, bringing down cobwebs and dust accumulated through the years, and painting the upper part. The result was great. My kitchen was bright and clean-smelling. I began thinking about a green living room and lavender bedroom.

Driving home in the Buick one day I realized the outside of the 713 needed something to relieve that monotonous red. "Monday," I asked, "why not some yellow trim on the windows?" He was all in favor if it meant another trip uptown to buy the paint.

Back home again we had lunch, Monday and I, and then I dug in the tool car for a ladder. I'd have to be careful and not fall; Bill would have a fit. By late afternoon I had all the window frames on one side painted a nice yellow. Wouldn't Bill be surprised!

I was cleaning the brushes when a shiny new motorcar stopped a few tracks away. Two men who looked like officials came walking over. Monday told them off so belligerently I had to lock him in the tool car.

"Who's outfit is this?" a big man with glasses asked.

"Fisher, signal department," I said. "Are you the signal supervisor?"

"No. Who painted those window frames yellow?"

"I did," I said happily. "Doesn't it make our old car look better?"

"Humph!" He walked around the outfit glowering. The other official stood between the tracks glowering. Then they both got on the motorcar and went puttering away in a very unfriendly manner.

I wondered if I'd done something wrong. They surely couldn't object to the yellow trim on our windows. It was a big improvement.

Bill came stomping in that evening and slammed his gloves on the floor. "Katheryne!" he demanded. "Did you paint our window frames yellow?"

"Yes, I did it today. Don't they look nice?"

"Read this!" He shoved a telegram under my nose.

"Well, you don't have to act so angry, I . . ."

"Read it."

"OFFICE SIG SUPV TO W FISHER COLFAX: DIV ENGR REPORTS SIG OUTFIT WITH YELLOW TRIM ON WINDOWS   PLEASE REFER TO RULE 638 AND ADVISE WHEN YOU HAVE REMOVED YELLOW PAINT   SIGNED B R BROWNING"

"I'm sorry. I just thought . . ."

"Kay, on the railroad you don't think! You've got me in the doghouse clear up to the General Office."

"Just because I painted the windows?"

"Because you changed the standard color from red," he fumed. "If you want to change the whole course of history, go right ahead. But don't try to change the railroad."

That evening he located some standard official boxcar red and painted over my nice yellow-trimmed windows. There was no romance in our bedroom that night. I lay in bed wondering how long it would take to learn all those crazy restrictions.

West Applegate in June. It was a cozy foothill community with a small motel, postoffice and general store alongside the main highway, only a block from the tracks. We arrived well before the outfits and Bill explored the rusty spur track. The area was level clean gravel which looked good to me but Bill fretted about the crossing wigwag being so close.

"Bet they won't push us beyond that road crossing because of the gravel in the flangeways. Wish I had a pick handy. Rather be further up the track."

"Bill," I said, "look at that shack over there. It's made of two old boxcar bodies without wheels set side by side."

"Probably a trackwalker's house. Must be a big family, judging from all the clothes on the line."

A school bus had stopped and several Mexican children came walking toward the shack singing "I'm a Yankee Doodle Dandy . . ." Monday went trotting over happily and was promptly chased back by a black dog three times his size. "Jim Two, no. No!" they all shouted.

I walked over to them. "Why do you call your dog Jim Two?" I asked.

The older girl informed me. "Our uncle owns his brother dog. His name is Jim. Our dog was second to be borned so he is Jim Two."

That's how I met Maria Francesca Guadalupe, the lady who lived in the boxcar house. She was hardly as large as her name, with a young face, beautiful black hair and smooth dark skin.

"I'm Kay," I explained. "Are these children all your family?"

"Oh, yes. I have one more not in school yet. Come in. I will make coffee." She pronounced it 'coffay'.

The shanty was nothing more than the two old car bodies patched together. One served as a kitchen and living space. The other, reached by a passage left when the side doors were removed, was one large bedroom. A curtain divided off one end, apparently where she and her husband slept. Only four small windows lighted the entire arrangement, but it all was clean as a pin, as were the children.

"How do you feed and take care of all this family?" I wondered.

"Oh, it's easy," she assured me. "Even Jim Two is fat. Only time we have trouble is when my husband drinks too much beer. Then we run out of money."

She hadn't understood. I meant, how did she stand the work, the endless cooking and washing dishes. I'd noticed the washing machine standing outside, covered with a canvas. I thought about the bedroom with its bunkbeds and a statuette of Our Saviour on a shelf, and wondered if the older children had witnessed the conception of their brothers and sisters. But all of that was of no concern to her. Only the money.

"How did you learn English so well?" I asked her.

"I come from Los Angeles. I even played in a movie once. But is better here. Good place for the kids."

Forty feet from the railroad track!

"We are lucky my husband is trackwalker," she explained. "We get a nice house." She was very happy.

When the outfits arrived Bill had an urgent discussion with the train crew about pushing the cars back farther from the wigwag. They left the 713 fifty feet from the wigwag and departed. He and the helper chopped the gravel out of the flangeways and he fussed for a week trying to get the cars moved. They remained right where they were.

There was some advantage in being so close to the road crossing; the ding-donging woke us up at night so we were prepared for the blasting whistle as each train rolled by only fifty feet from our door. We had to keep the windows open because of the warm weather, so each time our room was filled with smoke from the hot wheels.

But I did not complain. Maria had withstood it for years and would for many more to come. I wondered how she could be so happy.

One afternoon the dinging started and I heard the train coming, but instead of the two long, one short, one long blast of the whistle I heard "toot-toot-toot"; the signal for something on the track. I looked out as the engine charged by, but saw nothing unusual. Then a few minutes later Maria's girl, Ramona, was at my door.

"Our dog was hit by train," she sobbed. "Our mother want you to help." What could I do for an injured dog? I thought. The sight of blood frightened me. But I had learned that the Mexican people had a doctrine which dictated that you, if more able and capable than they in case of need, were obligated to help if they asked.

The dog was lying in the weeds gasping and whimpering, one shoulder badly mangled. The children were all crying.

Maria said, "I cannot leave the little ones or drive our car, Miss Kay. Do you think you can take him to hospital?"

"Maria . . . I don't know . . . he's bleeding and . . ."

She said something quickly in Spanish. Her boy Juan ran to the house and returned with the canvas from the washing machine. "We can put this on the back seat of your car," Maria pleaded.

I brought the Buick around and all of us together managed to get Jim Two into the rear seat. Maria again clicked off instructions in rapid Spanish. "Three of the oldest will go with you," she explained, "in order to hold him down."

During the eight miles to town only soft anxious voices came from the three Guadalupes kneeling on the floor in back caressing their dog. At the veterinarian's I went in and explained my problem, so he came outside. With everybody holding a corner of the canvas we carried poor Jim Two in and put him on a table. As the vet probed, the moaning dog struggled to rise.

"Abajo, Jeem," Ramona ordered. Jim Two layed back down. "He doesn't understand English," the worried girl explained.

"That's a fine how-do-you-do," the vet observed. Then he announced his diagnosis. "Fractured shoulder and a couple of ribs. He'll have to stay here for several days. But before you go," he added, "tell me that word again. Write it down."

Jim Two was gone more than a week, while Monday took over his duties of greeting the Guadalupe children as they got off the school bus each day. When the big dog returned home they became great pals.

Clipper Gap was the next move and that was the nicest location of all. We were coupled to a big track gang again but a different one, so I didn't get to see Cooky and Mr. Candy. The whole string of cars were pushed onto a long spur track that had once served a Hercules Powder plant. Now unused, it was separated from the mainline by a low hill so we escaped the noise and smoke and there were tall pine trees to shade the cars. Our front door looked onto a county road and some section houses with lush gardens and flowers.

But we stayed there only two weeks, then we and the track gang moved to Rocklin. Here the railroad finally reached the valley floor and leveled out. We were right beside the mainline again and the down trains, after their long descent of 7000 feet rolled through town with wheels pouring off smoke. The eastbound trains blasted by at fifty miles an hour as their three huge Mallets took a run at "the hill" with black clouds of smoke trailing behind.

The town was nice, with US 40 and stores only a block away but there were three street crossings so all trains blasted their whistles almost continuously as they charged through. For me, Rocklin was dusty, smoky, and noisy.

Newcastle in July. We were really doing our winter work in the hot foothill country. Trying to cook with the big coal stove made the outfit like an oven. We dusted off the old lawn chairs from the tool car and ate in the shade of a fruit warehouse. I used cold cuts as much as possible or cooked roasts early in the morning, letting them cool and serving with potato salads.

The station agent was Bill Flynn, a friendly, overweight gray-haired gentleman who looked more like a Senator than a telegrapher. He kept his office spic and span and suggested to Bill that we could string some wires from the outfit to his station so we'd have enough power to run the refrigerator. No matter if the temperature reached a hundred degrees Mr. Flynn always wore a white shirt and necktie.

Newcastle was a small picturesque town built right on top of a hill. Since it was only a forty-five minute drive from Sacramento I phoned and persuaded Aunty to drive up for a day and bring the kids. They were thrilled with our home on a railroad track and climbed over the 787 playing train. I had washed that morning and hung the clothes on a rope stretched from the baggage car to a post of the fruit shed. The children wanted me to take it down because it spoiled the looks of our 'train'. In the afternoon we all walked the one block to town for some shopping. When we came back the 713 was gone!

"Kay!" Aunty cried. "They're taking your home away." A switch engine was backing off through the yard with our two cars. A brakeman was holding up one end of my loaded clothesline.

"Sorry," he said, "but we gotta spot some reefers on this track. Have your outfit back pretty soon."

"That's all right," I assured him. "Just let me relieve you of those sheets before they get dirty." I calmed Aunty while we sat in the shade, with the laundry piled on a newspaper. The engine backed in and out with several yellow fruit cars. Finally it brought the 713 and 787 back and left them right where they'd been. The brakeman put up the steps and everything was normal.

"I wouldn't stand for it," Aunty declared. "I'd tell them to take their box cars somewhere else."

"You don't tell the railroad, Aunty. It tells you. No harm done. I suppose they'll be back tomorrow to get those cars."

There was some harm done. The cobblestone pot, which I'd left on the drainboard, had slid off into the sink and chipped a large piece from the spout. It always poured a little to one side after that.

"Bill," I said one day, "do you know we've been in this outfit one year?"
"We have?"

"And when are we going to bid out?"

"This fall, I hope. You know I'm just as anxious as you are."

I watched every job bulletin as it came out and saw them assigned to signalmen with five or ten years rights. Bill had just over one year. Almost hopelessly I realized the 713 was moving back up in the mountains. We were on our way to do our 'summer' work in the wintertime.

And I received a startling letter from Madge: *"Dear Kay: Sure sorry I been so long in writing. I guess you heard I divorced Roscoe and married Johnny Beavers. So now I'm Madge Beavers! Don't that knock your pants off? Roscoe was a nice guy, and he finally got the district job he wanted. But anyway, now Johnny has our outfit, me and him, and . . ."*

In October we were at Cisco again. Roy Ramgaw got sick and his district came open. I breathed down Bill's neck as he wrote out a bid for the position. When the bulletin came we read: "Truckee Maintainer assigned to B. Mackay, seniority date 3/12/39."

"Well, we're getting closer," Bill said.

"But when?" I cried.

"I don't know. Spring, maybe." He didn't want to guess. "Kay-Kay, I've been reading about a kind of chemical toilet. Maybe we could get one and put it in the tool car."

I looked out the window at the dreamhouse and the frost on the fir trees. "No, I don't like the idea."

"Why not?"

"Because it would mean we are getting set for another year."

"Aw, Kay-Kay."

He was restless that night. I felt sorry for him, worrying about facing another winter — or accepting the alternative of living apart.

November. Snow swirled around the outfit on Thanksgiving Day. Bill had been working like a beaver to get the work done so we could move lower down. The helper thought Bill was the worst boss he'd ever seen. Christmas week we moved to Towle spur, almost out of the snow territory.

We went down to Aunty's on New Year's Eve, and drove back late the next evening. It was cold and blustery as we mounted the tilted steps in the darkness.

"Damn place will be like an icebox," Bill said. "Hm, Joe Ramirez has been here." A brown company-mail envelope was stuck in the door. Inside the outfit he turned on a light, read the enclosed paper and left it lying on his desk. "Better keep your coat on until I get a fire going."

The paper on his desk looked like a bulletin.

"Bill Fisher, did you see this? Why didn't you tell me?" The typed words said: "Emigrant Gap Maintainer, assigned to W. Fisher, seniority date 7/1/41."

"Didn't think I'd get it." He had a scoop of coal in one hand but he put the other arm around me tightly. "I hid the other bulletin so you wouldn't be disappointed if we missed out."

"It's wonderful! When can we move?"

He explained we'd have to wait until his job was bid and assigned, probably within three weeks.

On the fifteenth of January the local stopped at Towle, the engine moved into the spur and trundled our cars out onto the main line to be coupled into the train. We watched them disappear up the track, then with Monday leading, we walked over to the Buick. A little while later we were standing beside the tracks at Emigrant Gap looking at our new home. Some of the track men were there to help unload our things when the train arrived.

By evening we were moved in, at least the furniture was scattered about the living room. There were no curtains on the windows, or pictures on the cream-colored tongue-and-groove walls. We had managed only to get the bed set up and the stoves working.

But we were alone! Beyond that door was a real bathroom, and here was a real kitchen, and a living room with big tall windows, and over our heads a true ceiling. We went to bed knowing that at last we were on solid ground, not rails.

"Bill," I whispered, "do you know what day this is?"

"You don't have to whisper now, Kay."

I laughed, "I forgot. But what day is it?"

"Hey, it's our wedding anniversary!" He turned over to kiss me, the kiss I had been waiting for a long time. Suddenly, in the other room, a telephone jangled. "What the hell?" he growled.

"You mean somebody is calling us now?"

"Guess so." He rolled out of bed, groping for a flashlight. In the next room I heard him lift the receiver. "Yes . . . I'm the new maintainer . . . Yes . . . All right . . ." He came shuffling back. "Kay, I've got a trouble call."

"Well, can't it wait until morning?"

"Signal trouble can't wait. I'll have to go." He searched for his clothes, prowling around so as not to turn on many lights. When he was ready he leaned over the bed to kiss me. "I don't know how long it will take. You'd better go to sleep."

I heard the front door shut as he went out. Happy Anniversary! Tears came to my eyes. Then I sat up in bed and jerked on the light. The house was silent and empty.

"Damn the railroads!" I said to the walls. "Damn the s.b. s.b. railroads."

17. Forty Years

Bill did come home from the trouble call about two AM and we had our second honeymoon after all. Even at two o'clock in the morning it was like heaven to be in the privacy of our own bedroom, with a dim light burning and the world of trains and squeaky steel cots well beyond the securely locked front door.

I was to learn that these trouble calls would be forever frequent and unexpected; in the dark of a snowy night, in the middle of a Sunday dinner, or on a summer afternoon when friends were visiting. Once he even was called out just as neighbors were dropping in for a surprise birthday party I'd planned for him. But that was all in the future.

The next day I started by pushing our meager furniture around, planning for a rug to cover the worn linoleum, pictures to hang on the tongue-and-groove walls, some table lamps. In a few days the sun came out bright on the snow that still lay on the ground, gleaming through the tall windows. I was a little lonesome for my poor canary, he would have enjoyed it. The cookstove burned coal but it was small, shiny, and easy to control compared to the slow monster in the outfit. Plenty of crystal clear water gushed from the faucets at a touch and I realized I had a habit of being frugal with water, worrying about how much might be in the tanks. The radio worked great and I kept it going constantly.

The community was small, all railroad families, and we made many friends. The track foreman's wife next door started teaching me how to cook Mexican dishes. The trains still pounded past day and night a hundred feet from the house, but I knew that never again could one of those locomotives couple onto our domicile and drag it away.

March was cold and windy, with intermittent snow flurries, but our bedroom was cozy and so was the spacious warm bathroom! Bill usually got home for a hot lunch now and surely appreciated them. Only occasionally, when he knew he'd be too far away at noon did we dust off the battered lunch bucket. One noon he came home, stomping off the snow on the front porch.

"Hiya, wife," he greeted happily. "Guess what, the 713 is moving into the spur here today."

"You don't mean it!" I was all questions. Who had the job now? Did he have a wife with him in the outfit? I thought, at least they are coming in daylight, even though it was spitting snow. I remembered the gruesome night when we'd walked out of Troy and arrived here wet and frozen, to find the outfits were somewhere else.

"All I know, " Bill said, "is that his name is Byron Sanders and he's going to help me with some pole line work for a week or two."

As he was finishing lunch we heard the engine of "deloco" outside. He hurried out while I stood at the window and watched. The engine moved into the snow buried spur track against the hillside a few hundred yards from our house, plowing a deep trench. Then it backed out and disappeared, no doubt to retrieve the cars from down at the telegraph office.

Soon it was back again, pushing the 713 and sagging 787 boxcar slowly up to the end of the trench. The banks of snow hid the wheels and as the engine departed, they where alone like two forgotten old barges in a backwash bay. Bill and another man were already at work digging a trench in the snow to string out water hoses and wires for lights. I thought how many times he'd done that, he'd know how for sure.

At dinner I was anxious for more news.

"Well, I guess he has a wife," Bill offered. "Didn't say what her name was. He's gone to Colfax on a helper to get his car. Kind of worried if his wife will stay in the outfit."

Next day I watched for signs of life. No lights showed in the old baggage car, only a thin wisp of smoke drifted from the tin stovepipe, as if Mr. Sanders had gone to work and let his fires go out. Poor thing, I thought, she probably got one look at this snow and went back home to Mom. Or maybe they rented a house somewhere and he's batching up here. I could hardly wait for Bill to come home with more information.

"Byron's a good guy," he offered. "Darned good lineman, hard worker. Just got out of the army a few months ago."

"But is his wife in the outfit?" I persisted.

"Darned if I know. Didn't ask him."

Men! The next day I decided to find out. Bundled against the persistent, blustering snow flurries I tramped up the track with Monday bouncing along ahead. How familiar it felt! The 713 seemed to tip its tin stovepipe in welcome, but there was no sound, no footprints on the portable steps. I realized there was no dreamhouse standing in the snow with a tribulation trail leading to it.

I climbed the steps anyway and banged on the door, thinking of Madge Nichols, or Beavers it was now. After a second try, the door opened a crack. I could see a young woman's face. "Hello, I'm Kay Fisher," I said. "Are you Mrs. Sanders?"

The door opened a little farther so I went in. The girl was in a bathrobe, standing wide-eyed in the middle of the dark kitchen. She was short and chubby, with a round face and large dark eyes like those of Spanish people. But she seemed to be speechless.

"I walked over to visit you," I explained. "I'm your neighbor,"

"You walked . . . in this snow to see me?" She was incredulous.

"Yes, of course. I'm used to snow. I lived in this car until a few months ago."

She stared in disbelief. "I never saw snow before!" she exclaimed. "I didn't know anybody could walk in it, at least a woman. I'm afraid if I go outside I'll freeze or get lost." She wandered dazedly into the living room and turned on the overhead light.

The room appeared barren without our overstuffed chair and sofa. The little desk by the window was the same, the pot-bellied stove, the steel cot at the far end, now covered with boxes as if it wasn't being used. The stove was stone cold. "Why don't you have a fire going?" I asked.

"I can't make it work, Mrs. . . . Kay, you said? I been staying in bed since I got here."

I had a basket case for sure! I looked at her feet, blue with chill in flimsy slippers. "Tell you what," I began. "Oh, what's your name?"

"Carmelita, but Byron calls me Carmelly. He says it doesn't sound so much like Mexican. I'm Portugese."

"Tell you what, Carmelita, you put on some long warm stockings if you have any and I'll get your fire going."

I found some kindling in the kitchen and the same old kerosene can. The coal bucket in the living room was full. As she came out of the bedroom I was digging in the stove with the poker, ignoring the usual cloud of ashes. I stuffed in paper and kindling, getting soot on my hand, slopped in the kerosene and a generous amount of coal. When I tossed in the match the mixture went "woof" and Carmelita jumped.

"Just go easy on the kerosene," I advised her.

"How did you know all about that stove?" she said in amazement.

I thought of Cisco, and Troy, and Corral Track Five, of Thatcher Kelly, Dora Terroli, Madge. I remembered Millie Smith and my canary, snowstorms and summer heat, and decided I'd better break in Carmelly Sanders slowly lest she die of shock. In a minute the pot-bellied stove was roaring nicely and the tin pipe becoming cherry red color.

"Well," I suggested, "let's get the kitchen stove going. I'll supervise and you go through the motions."

The big cookstove was more massive than I remembered. I deftly lifted off the lids with the iron bar and dug in the grates, wondering if the Parson's special pipe still leaked. I knew I was doing it all correctly because the proper amount of ashes drifted up. With my help Carmelita got a reasonable fire laid, spilling the normal amount of coal on the floor. Then, I don't know if it was just time, or being in the 713 again. . . .

"Carmelly," I asked, "where is your dreamhouse?"

"Dreamhouse?" She looked completely blank.

"Oh, I'm sorry. Your toilet."

"Here in this other car," she answered, as if I should know. She opened the end door, letting a flurry of snow. The same skittery plank connected with the 787's door. Inside, right next to the coal bin was a new cubicle and a patent chemical toilet. "I just hate this cold place," Carmelita told me.

I decided not to mention our old dreamhouse and that right in this same spot the roof had blown off with me inside!

Coming out of the 787 across the plank I heard Monday saying, "Yap-yap-yap." He looked up between the couplings at me.

"Monday, I forgot all about you." And then to Carmelly, "Do you mind if I let my dog come in?" And since she didn't mind, to Monday I said, "Go to the steps, go to the steps." He was there when I opened the side door, bounced in and excitedly went smelling around his old home.

With both fires going and the outfit getting warm, I sat with Carmelita in the caboose chairs in the living room and we talked. She was amazed that I was so self-sufficient and natural in such weird surroundings. I tried hard to encourage her without mentioning the rough parts, thinking of Madge showing me how to get the steps out and Emma Ramgaw who must have experienced worse things than I did.

Trudging back to my house that afternoon, I realized how Bill and I had made it to the first limb on the tall seniority tree and Carmelita and Byron

Kay, Bill and their dog in front of the signal maintainer's house at Emigrant Gap.
(From a postcard)

Sanders were now on the bottom. Next day I went to see her again, taking along an extra pair of overshoes, and showed her how to tuck slacks into the tops so the snow wouldn't get in. I brought her to my house and we visited in the bright kitchen, where I told her about my cobblestone pot now serving as a planter on the table.

When the weather cleared a few days later I took her down to Mrs. Merrithew's telegraph office. She was frantic as we came to the short section of snowsheds but I tramped along like it was the normal thing to do. Edith Merrithew encouraged her too, and entertained her with stories of by-gone days on the railroad.

Then in two weeks they were gone, on their way to Truckee. I hoped they didn't get spotted on Shop Track One. When I wondered about there being no helper with them Bill explained that Byron would work with different maintainers until the rail laying started in May. I prayed that Carmelita would survive the squeaky steel cot.

Spring came in May and with it wild daffodils appeared among the remaining snow banks, now blackened with train soot. In a few weeks the knarled manzanita bushes displayed their blossoms and the fir trees had bright green growth at the tips of the limbs. A letter came from Carmelita saying Byron had taken a job in Nevada and they would be living in a house. I was glad she escaped the outfit car in such a short time.

The railroad was swamped with wartime traffic as train after train loaded with fighting equipment rolled through night and day. Passenger trains crowded with GIs, sometimes a dozen sections in one day, went clattering past. That was the sad part for we knew that many of them would never come back. Bill worked seven days a week, often sixteen hours. He said traffic had reached a peak of fifty trains a day.

The track foreman next door, his crew now increased to forty men, asked for a Clerk-Timekeeper and suggested me for the job. Then I realized how just keeping the track in shape against pounding trains and shortage of material was a stupendous job, and I soon learned about switch points, rail, angle bars, frogs, how to order a carload of coal or hurriedly write a hospital order for a man hurt.

One requirement of the job was that I ride out with the crew each morning and check off the men after the work had started. This meant climbing aboard their big track motorcar pulling several trailers of workers and tools in the crisp dawn. The Mexican laborers called me "Kayco" and kidded me about spelling their names incorrectly. My vocabulary of Spanish words became well rounded. Once the check-off was complete and I had talked over my duties for the day with the foreman, I hitched a ride back to my little 'office' at his house on the first available helper engine. I learned how to light a fusee and stand in plain view near the track to signal a "pick me up" to an approaching light engine.

The engine crews soon knew me and when an engine stopped the fireman would reach down for my tin box of papers while I scrambled expertly up the iron ladder, often thinking of Madge's first lesson. Up on the oily deck he'd dust off the head brakeman seat next to the front windows away from the roaring firebox and huge boiler head with its myriad of valves and gauges. The trainmen appreciated that I was doing my share to help keep the railroad running.

Riding on one of the Mallets was a real thrill. The pounding wheels and rods, the very massiveness and throbbing heartbeat of the locomotive seemed to symbolize the whole realm of railroading. Sometimes when track men were in sight ahead the engineer would let me blow the majestic echoing whistle, warning of our approach. I learned how to space the first two long blasts and the short one, then taper off the final long with my personal "English". And I felt the urgency and dedication of these men and my husband in staying on a job that might pay less than others but held a fascination, a sense of duty.

Then one sparkling summer day beyond my office window I noticed "deloco" coming west with a dozen or so cars, and one looked familiar. There just ahead of the caboose was the 713 without her constant old companion, the 787. The short train stopped opposite the house to do some switching so I walked out and across the tracks.

She looked forlorn and forgotten. Two windows were broken out, tilted stovepipe missing, the paint was chipped and around the window ledges it had peeled off to show the yellow I once put there. Tacked onto the side was a placard lettered DESTINATION — Scrap Yard. So this was her last trip. She had served her time for perhaps fifty years, first as a baggage and mail car in the passenger trains of her day, and then for years a traveling home for no-telling how many aspiring employees.

With a hiss of airbrakes the train began to move. I walked alongside and patted her weathered side boards. "Goodbye, old girl . . . and thanks."

When Bill came home and I gave him the news he looked at me for a long minute. Then he said, "You know, that was silly of me to put up those lace curtains. You remember your first night in the baggage car?"

"I'll never forget it!" I hugged him tightly. "But the lace curtains were not silly, dear. They kept our marriage together and I think it's going to last a long time."

As I write this final page, it has lasted over forty years.

There is much more to tell — of little Monday, a true railroad dog who lived fourteen years, of a family that came along, and of the trains.

The heavy traffic during the war years, overworked crews, snow and snow-bound trains, derailments, the track men who often worked many hours without relief, their families, heroic acts that went unrecorded, the small incidents that in one way or another kept the trains moving, the signalmen, linemen, telegraphers, dispatchers, and yes, the officials who directed their men, often around the clock in emergencies — all comprise a story that we hope can be told another time.

Sad but inevitable was the phase-out of the great steam locomotives. Those people who designed, built, repaired, operated, rerailed, loved and lived with those magnificent machines were a part of railroad history for a hundred years. We are proud to have been among them.

For the Railbuff: By the 1930s almost all of the cab-forward Mallet engines on this route had been rebuilt to single-expansion AC types, and the newer articulated engines were being built to the AC design. However, everyone on the railroad still referred to them as the "mallees" until the end of steam.

Typography by Joseph Halton, Alta, California
This book was set on a Model 5 linotype in 10 point Century Schoolbook. The chapter heads were set by hand in 14 point Craw Modern Bold. Cover title was hand set in in Post Old Style Condensed.

Thanks to these good friends who encouraged and helped
us to publish this book —

Roberta Bryant
Bob Church
Roger Levenson
Jim Bassett
Ida

Kay and Bill